Other books by Gostick and Elton

The Carrot Principle
The Invisible Employee
A Carrot a Day
The 24-Carrot Manager

Books by Gostick and Dana Telford

The Integrity Advantage
Integrity Works

Book by Gostick and Scott Christopher

The Levity Effect

The Daily
Carrot
Principle

365 Ways to Enhance Your
Career & Life

Adrian Gostick
and Chester Elton

with Scott Christopher, Andrea Gappmayer,
and Chris Kendrick

Free Press
New York   London   Toronto   Sydney

_f_P

FREE PRESS
A Division of Simon & Schuster, Inc.
1230 Avenue of the Americas
New York, NY 10020

First Free Press hardcover edition April 2010

FREE PRESS and colophon are trademarks of Simon & Schuster, Inc.

For information about special discounts for bulk purchases,
please contact Simon & Schuster Special Sales at 1-866-506-1949
or business@simonandschuster.com

The Simon & Schuster Speakers Bureau can bring authors
to your live event. For more information or to book an event contact
the Simon & Schuster Speakers Bureau at 1-866-248-3049
or visit our website at www.simonspeakers.com.

Manufactured in the United States of America

1   3   5   7   9   10   8   6   4   2

Library of Congress Cataloging-in-Publication Data

Gostick, Adrian Robert.
The daily carrot principle : 365 ways to enhance your career & life /
by Adrian Gostick and Chester Elton.
p. cm.
1. Employee motivation. 2. Corporate culture. I. Elton, Chester. II. Title.
HF5549.5.M63G668 2010
650.1—dc22
2009052234

ISBN 978-1-4391-8173-7

Dedicated to our remarkable teammates.
You taught us so many of the principles
we share in these pages.

Our deepest thanks to:

Christy Chatelain
Kim Coxey
Scott Christopher
Andrea Gappmayer
Steve Gibbons
Andrew Hahn
BobAnn Hall
Angie Haugen
Chris Kendrick
Todd Nordstrom
Pat Poyfair
Stephanie Rodriguez

INTRODUCTION

As often as three times a day, young Stoyan Palazov takes his place on the lower end of a circus teeterboard, a long plank with one end raised. Lights and music swirl around him as he waits for two burly performers to leap onto the board's other end, rocketing him more than twenty feet into the air, which is how he will land on the shoulders of his brother, the apex of a five-man tower.

If the young man lands a few inches too far forward or back, he will topple everyone. His landing must be perfectly balanced or he ruins the act; which, he admits with a little smile, he has done more than a few times since he began performing at age eleven. "Everyone [makes] mistakes," Stoyan said. "I am learning."

Stoyan's unique situation makes one wonder about his first attempt as a boy, and his second. How does a boy with two feet planted firmly on the ground progress to the point where he can fly through the air at dizzying heights, flipping and landing with perfect ease? For that matter, how does anyone take that first leap into the unknown?

The business people we meet around the world don't ask that question, exactly; but when you boil it down, *that's* what we all really want to know. Rarely a day goes by that we are not asked, "How do I get started?" Translation: How do I take myself, my team, my business to the soaring heights of the great workplaces and successful individuals you describe—without landing on my head?

We wrote *The Daily Carrot Principle* to answer these questions. To smooth the learning curve inherent in effectively using the Carrot Principle, we divided the concepts into an easily digestible format that builds your knowledge step by step and day by day. An I.T. employee told us he read one page of our first one-a-day book, *A Carrot a Day*, in the morning while his computer was powering up. Then he would work on the new concept all day. He didn't sense the magnitude of his daily efforts until one day, when he looked around and found he and those around him were operating at a different altitude. "It was startling, but exhilarating," he said.

In the world of acrobatics, that's what you'd call a perfect landing. Taking a leap of faith and then hitting your mark "feels good," Stoyan says. "It feels like you are the king!"

Having an experienced guide to help him navigate through practice was key to Stoyan's achievement. That's why we've created this book: to be with you every step of the way as you begin to use, or continue to use, the Carrot Principle. If you read just one page a day, by the end of the year you'll have been exposed to all the concepts of our best-selling series, augmented with new comments and explanations, and thoughts from great thinkers on management. A daily "Action" on each page will lead you through implementing each concept with precision and prevent any wrong turns as you learn to:

- Set clear goals
- Communicate effectively
- Build trusting relationships
- Hold yourself accountable for results
- Recognize the great work of others

Soon, you will discover that you have made a transition; instead of following the guide, you will discover that you are setting the pace for others. It's a natural progression for those who are committed to their craft of business.

Practice, Practice

We learned once of a fisherman, Dai Lewis, who taught himself to fly fish by putting a book between his elbow and his body while casting. If the book fell, it meant that the casting action was inaccurate—the elbow was moving and he wasn't holding everything in a straight line. His practice made his cast almost perfect, resulting in a line that was never too straight or too slack, and a fly that would drop onto the water just in front of the fish without showing much line. Like the most effective people in any venture, Lewis loved his craft and was committed to mastering his art. Sure, his work was unusual (some might call it play), but work does not have to be exotic to be loved.

Masters of any craft are passionate, and with the help of an experienced guide they work tirelessly to improve their abilities. Whether your work is fishing, triple flips, or serving customers, if you commit to practice and follow an experienced guide, you will achieve more—and others will follow you.

Take this example. A few years ago, Chester was coaching his son's basketball team in the Summit, New Jersey rec. league. The teams were made up of ten- and eleven-year-olds, and exactly no one was going on to the National Basketball Association. Believing in the importance of the

Carrot Principle, Chester and his team started the season by coming up with a list of collective goals including, "We never criticize a teammate" (after all, no one wants to mess up), "Everyone cheers" (on the court and on the bench), "No hanging on the rim after dunking" (for fun, since not a single player was over four-foot-five), and "Everyone scores" (much more interesting than "Everyone plays").

One of Chester's less-coordinated players was James, freshly emigrated from England. James played the cello beautifully, but had never played a game of basketball in his life. Without assistance, or a stepladder, James had little chance of scoring a basket, so Chester assigned his talented point guard, Patrick, the task of helping James succeed. "A great point guard makes others better," Chester explained to Patrick. "And if you can help James score a basket, then you are really good. So get James in position and feed him the ball until he scores."

There was no doubt that capable Patrick loved basketball. He had benefited from experienced coaches to guide his practice, and now was ready to use his abilities to make his teammate successful.

When James finally hit a shot, the team and stands went wild. James's mom greeted Chester after the game with tears in her eyes. She was unable to express more than a simple, "thank you." Neither mom nor son would ever forget the moment, and neither would Patrick, the point guard who made it happen. In that moment, he experienced the highest form of success: lifting yourself by lifting others.

The Daily Carrot Principle is about moments like this. It's about making you, and everyone around you, better. In writing this book, we pictured ourselves standing with you on the brink of a giant leap forward. Our goal from here is to guide you through the precision twists and turns of using the Carrot Principle. Along the way, we hope to inspire a love and commitment to improving your skills. And in the end, we promise that there will be an undeniable moment of realization when you will look around and discover that you have landed on your feet and are operating at an entirely different altitude. Most important, you will realize that rather than following, you have, remarkably, become the guide.

The Daily
Carrot
Principle

Dream Big

*Dream no small dreams for they have no power
to move the hearts of men.*
—Goethe

In a cab ride in New York City, we struck up a conversation with the driver. He had an eastern European accent, so we were curious as to how he ended up in the Big Apple. When we asked, he told us that he left Romania during the reign of Nicolae Ceauşescu, risking everything. Why did he do it, sleeping on the streets and saving pennies to bring his family to America? His explanation: "You have something here that we don't have in Romania. Something I want for my children . . . dreams!"

Dreams and ambitions can sometimes get a bad rap today. It's easy to discount the former as childish and the latter as greedy. That's a mistake. In a way, troubled times can make it easier for people to reorient their priorities. If there was ever a time to dream big, it is today. When the rest of the world says hunker down and try to survive, we say that it is time to thrive.

So go ahead and dream. A dream is a powerful motivator.

CARROT ACTION: Make a list of your successes. Then make goals for this year that will build on that momentum.

The Effectiveness of Praise

How the encouragement of others propels us forward.

In 1925, Dr. Elizabeth Hurlock conducted a study with a group of fourth and sixth grade math students in the United States. She wanted to see whether their output could be modified, not by the content of the lessons but by the feedback they received as they solved problems. The control group was praised for their efforts; another was criticized; and a third ignored. Hurlock measured their improvement by the number of math problems they solved each day.

The results were immediate. By the second day, the "praised" students dramatically outperformed the rest. At the end of the five-day study, the results were in: the students increased the number of solved problems in direct relation to the level of encouragement they received.

- Praised students: +71%
- Criticized students: +19%
- Ignored students: +5%

Praise works! Whether in the classroom, office, or other work site, people need encouragement to do their best work.

CARROT ACTION: In a journal, write down an experience in your life in which someone encouraged and praised you, and by doing so motivated you to achieve something great.

Who Do You Trust?

Put not your trust in money, but put your money in trust.
—Oliver Wendell Holmes

Johnny Carson was the host of the television game show *Who Do You Trust* in 1957. To play, couples were separated, and the husbands were given a category of the question they were to answer next. They had to either answer it or "trust" their wives to answer it. Ironically, that show aired during the quiz show scandal era, when it was discovered that the popular game show *The $64,000 Question* had scripted the loss of a contestant to allow a more popular contestant to win. The whistleblower? The losing player.

How much do you trust the people on your team? Given their different strengths, do you know which person will respond best to a particular challenge?

The curious thing about trust is that it presumes familiarity. You can't trust somebody you don't know. So the first step in establishing trust is getting to know the people around you. And equally important is letting other people come to know you.

CARROT ACTION: Boost levels of trust in your organization by using language that encourages it—for instance, express confidence in others' abilities to achieve their goals. Trust is also built as we get to know our colleagues outside the office. Once a month go out for drinks, dinner, or a movie together.

Thank You in Ninety Seconds

Instant Carrots.

⌒

The next time a co-worker helps you out, grab a thank-you card, a pen, and follow these steps to quick recognition:

Write a fun comment about that person and your relationship.

- *Dear Sue, How many times a day do I hear you say, "No problem?"*

Thank them for whatever it is you appreciate.

- *Thanks for picking up the phones for me this morning when I got called away.*

Tell them specifically how what they did helped you.

- *If you hadn't, we would probably have missed the call from Tom at TechnoTex, and I'm guessing he would have placed his order somewhere else.*

Tell her why what she did was important.

- *I appreciate your teamwork. If the company were full of Sues, the competition wouldn't stand a chance!*

CARROT ACTION: Take ninety seconds today to write a specific note of appreciation to someone who has helped you.

Failing Well

*I have not failed. I've just found
10,000 ways that won't work.*
—Thomas A. Edison

We love the story of Charles Goodyear and his invention of vulcanized rubber, which shockingly has nothing to do with Leonard Nimoy. It's the process that takes a common substance and transforms it into the thing that allows modern life to exist. Without rubber there would be no cars, bicycles, planes, or even our favorite pair of old sneakers.

The crazy thing about Goodyear's story is that the final breakthrough was a fluke. Angry with the people who mocked his latest failed experiments, he threw the rubber-sulfur mixture in his hand onto a nearby burning stove in disgust. When he went back to get it, he discovered that heat had cured the rubber. Eureka! In an instant, all of the struggle—his time in debtor's prison, the years of poverty and hunger—evaporated.

Later, Goodyear said that failure gave him information necessary to be able to recognize the meaning in the breakthrough.

That's a good concept to keep in mind in your business. The key is to embrace that unstable sensation. If it pans out, great; if not, try something else.

CARROT ACTION: Take a minute to review a few "failures" in your past. Note any positive outcomes from what seemed, at the time, like a disaster.

Who Am I?

Character is like a tree and reputation like its shadow.
The shadow is what we think of it;
the tree is the real thing.
—Abraham Lincoln

You probably have a hero or two. But do you think anybody wants to be like *you*?

You might be surprised.

Who we are and who other people assume we are can be quite distinct. You didn't get to choose many of your characteristics. That's where genetics comes in. But to a great extent you do get to choose the characteristics of your *reputation*.

From the moment you're hired, you begin to create your business reputation. The decisions you make, the things you say, the way you carry yourself, and an infinite number of tiny gestures all combine into a perception-version of yourself. It's a little intimidating to think of it in those terms, but that's how it works. The good news is it shouldn't be frightening. This is an opportunity to become the colleague you ideally want to be. Ultimately, your business reputation is largely a product of many small decisions.

CARROT ACTION: Compare in your mind how you perceive yourself versus how other people see you. Does your reputation need a bit of polishing?

Corporate Mutiny

You're taking the ship?
Yes, mutiny! Pass the word.
—*Mutiny on the Bounty,* 1935 film

In the King's navy, no word was more dangerous than "mutiny." The mere whisper of "mutiny" was a treasonous offense and its consequence swift: "Hang him from the yard arm!" Twenty-first century employees have it a bit differently. Sure, there are still admirals of industry and captains of commerce, but the balance of influence is radically different now. A successful organization today thrives on the input of many, even opposing, voices. Organizations invite debate as they make battle plans. A wise leader loves dissent . . . up to a point, of course.

When a strategy is put into place, the organization needs consensus to carry out the plan. This unity of purpose can be problematic for people, particularly for those who were on the other side of the argument before a plan was adopted. It is a leader's job to get everyone on board at this stage. Positive incentives are much more successful than threatening people's jobs, the corporate version of a gangplank.

CARROT ACTION: The next time you disagree with strategy, remember: it's okay if the plan doesn't ultimately sail; but it's not okay if you try to make it sink.

In It to Win It

The cure for boredom is curiosity.
There is no cure for curiosity.
—Dorothy Parker

Have you ever met somebody who was curious about everything? Someone who was always pushing the team to answer tough questions and grow? Despite the energy such thinking requires, curious people are overflowing with zeal to learn and to contribute the benefits of their learning to others.

We find in our work with global organizations that the people who are engaged make the best employees, the people who get the most promotions, raises, and attention. If you answer yes to the following six questions, there's a good chance you (and your team) are engaged.

My team is highly motivated to contribute to the success of the organization.

My team consistently looks for more efficient and effective ways to get the job done.

My team has a strong sense of personal accomplishment from its work.

My team understands how its roles help the organization meet its goals.

My team always has a positive attitude.

My manager does a good job of recognizing employee contributions.

CARROT ACTION: If you answered positively to five or six questions, you are highly engaged. If you said yes to four or less, it's time to reassess your commitment.

Great Expectations

To accomplish great things, we must dream as well as act.
—Anatole France

In 1954, a milestone in sports was achieved that no one had thought possible: the four-minute mile. When Roger Bannister cracked the barrier, the world erupted with excitement. They called it the miracle mile, and Bannister's face was everywhere. Surely, everyone thought, this inconceivable feat was a record that would stand for generations.

But it doesn't work that way.

The record stood for less than a month.

Soon, the four-minute mile became a benchmark of what a great runner should be capable of achieving. Other athletes knew that the bar had been raised. They also saw that Bannister was adored by millions, and his competitors wanted a piece of that kind of glory.

In every business there is a four-minute mile barrier, some ideal of service, innovation, or commitment that employees strive for and wonder if they'll ever actually meet. The fact to keep in mind is that over time what once seemed like miracles will become expectations. That's how progress works.

CARROT ACTION: If you had to write down your miracle accomplishment, your four-minute mile in business or in life, what would it be? Write it down and start running toward it.

All By Yourself?

Bring the walls down.

You go to work, park yourself in an upholstered cube in which you can touch all the walls at the same time, and you keep your eyes focused on a screen all day. At the end of the day, you march out the front door with colleagues you don't really know. Sad, right?

When employees are recognized in a public setting by gathering everybody together and praising the accomplishment of someone whose work benefited everyone, a curious thing happens: the walls fall down and relationships can form.

Recognition is an emotional release that is also a communal rite. It doesn't matter that you're not the one scoring the winning touchdown or grabbing the first-place ribbon. If you are present, part of the pride of working in a winning organization rubs off.

CARROT ACTION: Someone in your group of colleagues is probably feeling isolated right now. Find a way today to make that person feel like a valued member of your work community by publicly recognizing one of his strengths.

Office Love

Life's greatest happiness is to be convinced we are loved.
—Victor Hugo

Before we work with corporate groups, we send out surveys that ask employees to note the last time they were recognized for their good work. The majority of people we survey say it's been at least six months since their last public recognition moment, and about a third say it's been longer than a year.

Imagine if your spouse or significant other only said "I love you" once a year. How would that go over? Everyone understands the need for frequent recognition in our personal lives, but what about at work?

Remember that effective recognition is frequent. Your methods should vary from providing specific words of encouragement, to hand writing a note of thanks, to thanking a team member in a staff meeting, and so on.

Your personal relationships need "I love yous" and your business relationships need "thank yous." Just don't get the two mixed up.

CARROT ACTION: Make a goal to say "thank you" to each co-worker at least every seven days. It should be a public, verbal expression of your appreciation.

Trickle-Up

Never doubt that a small group of thoughtful,
committed citizens can change the world.
Indeed, it is the only thing that ever has.
—Margaret Mead

We've witnessed powerful results when corporations recognize and reward their employees, but some organizations just don't buy it. We know many managers haven't seen the light. They'll say, "My people don't care about that soft stuff. They get a paycheck. That's plenty."

No, it's not. Seventy-nine percent of workers who left their jobs said a lack of appreciation was a reason for quitting. A full 75 percent of the U.S. workforce is not fully engaged at work, and yet 90 percent say that the one thing that would convince them to commit to their organizations is (hint: it's not a raise) if their leaders recognized their hard work.

If you're one of the 90 percent, you might feel like there's little you can do, but the truth is that you have more influence than you think. It's partly up to you to change the culture.

Begin by recognizing co-workers when you see them achieve something great.

CARROT ACTION: If your boss isn't good at acknowledging your accomplishments, show him or her how you should be treated: praise a peer in front of them to help create a recognition environment on your team.

Turning Over

Pleasure in the job puts perfection in the work.
—Aristotle

There's a secret cost of doing business. It makes economists shiver when they talk about it. Surprisingly, it's not copy toner. It's the cost of replacing you.

The replacement cost for departing employees is vastly understated on corporate balance sheets. Traditionally, management estimates $5,000 or $6,000 for every lost employee, but recent studies blow that figure out of the water. When considering lost productivity, lost customers, the cost and time to hire and train your replacement, turnover actually equals 150 percent of your annual salary. In the United States, four million employees voluntarily leave their jobs every month. That's 48 million annually. With the national average salary of $34,065, the replacement of the churning workforce is $1.7 trillion every year (or roughly the cost of your kid's braces). The worldwide number, as you can project, is astronomical.

While that figure is horrible news for your employer, it's terrific news for you. Your loyalty is worth a lot to your organization.

CARROT ACTION: Just as you insure an object of value not by what it cost you but by what it would cost to replace it, bump up your own sense of employee worth by realizing your true replacement value. Use the formula above to calculate your true replacement value.

R-E-S-P-E-C-T

Sock-it-to-me, sock-it-to-me, sock-it-to-me, sock-it-to-me.

Time magazine reported in 2006 a statistic that too many of us have experienced firsthand: 80 percent of employees believe that they get no respect at work.

Let's change that. With your teammates, use vocabulary that is humanizing. Remember their names, say please and thank you, ask about their days. You work, and you might be a worker, but you're not a worker bee. You should also take care with your tone. Avoid raising your voice and keep a lightness to your speech.

Next, respect privacy. You deserve a little space, a bit of personal distance. Legally, of course, there are boundaries, but you also have a right to expect professional courtesy.

Here's another good one: you deserve to disagree. You want to foster or work in an environment that permits differing points of view.

Finally, you should feel safe at work—physically safe, obviously, and also emotionally safe. A good boss has your back. You have the right to expect him or her to protect you in that way.

CARROT ACTION: It's tricky to think of a response when suddenly confronted with disrespect by a co-worker or manager. So prepare yourself in advance. Take a minute to role-play. If someone has said or done things that you consider disrespectful, map out an appropriate response now.

Corporate Eyesight

Seeing opportunities.

Napoleon demanded a secret communication system because he wanted something to enable his soldiers to converse silently and even in the dark. In response to the request, Charles Barbier developed a code of raised dots on paper that spelled out words. The military rejected it, however, because it was too hard to learn.

So Barbier took his idea to the National Institute for the Blind in Paris. There, he met Louis Braille, who was blind. Braille fixed Barbier's system, modifying it so that the finger didn't have to travel to read a symbol. In the Braille system, any letter could be composed of six dots (1 to 3 in a column on the left, and 4 to 6 on the right) with a space between each letter. The letter M, for example, is composed of three raised dots, 1–3–4. Voilà: the invention of Braille, which revolutionized communication for millions.

Corporations also use visual vocabulary. They talk of a strategic corporate vision, clarity of goals, and a focus on excellence. Such talk is often as unclear to employees and as hard to learn as Barbier's early system. Such vague vision, goals, and focus must be followed by more in-depth communication; otherwise it's like you're wearing blinders.

CARROT ACTION: Don't be afraid to ask for clarification on corporate or team goals. Keep your comments centered on the needs of the organization.

Funny, How That Works

A lighten-up strategy.

While most ad agencies were downsizing during the recent recession, one public-relations agency, Peppercom, in New York, remained solid. The agency laid off only three of its seventy-person staff after the economy took a dive. One of its strategies was a reliance on an unconventional business tool: stand-up comedy.

The agency brings in a professional comedian for sessions lasting a few hours each to teach employees of all ranks how they can integrate the craft in their everyday jobs— showing that laughter's good for business, not to mention a way to boost happiness and motivation at work.

"It's probably the single smartest internal investment we've made in the agency," said Steve Cody, managing partner of Peppercom. In the stand-up sessions, young account executives and junior account executives at Peppercom hone their craft by developing confidence and poise for public speaking and dealing with clients. They're also finding that when you're funny, people pay attention.

CARROT ACTION: Find an appropriate (yes, appropriate) joke and spread some cheer around the office. Take note how people respond and modify your humor to fit the culture of your workplace.

Making Tough Decisions

What to do when faced with two roads diverging.

Doing the right thing in business is often clearer than it may first appear. Making a decision usually means taking one of two roads. In 95 percent of cases, taking one road is to do the right thing. To take the other road, you have to sit back and spin a story around the decision you are making or the action you are taking. If you find yourself thinking up an elaborate justification for what you're doing, you're probably not doing the right thing.

Of course, it would be naïve to think that there are no gray courses of action people can take or decisions they can make. But with the right counsel and the right alignment to your organization's core values, you usually make the right decision.

One of the marks of a trustworthy person is the ability to deliberate in making tough decisions. By debating with trusted colleagues, inevitably you'll end up with a black-and-white decision. As an individual, though, you may not be able to make such a clear choice.

CARROT ACTION: Despite differing views in some areas, one thing all the leaders we have met agree on is the need for good advisors. Form a group of trusted advisors that you can bounce tough decisions off. Look for people with high moral character and varied backgrounds.

Small kindnesses

Carrots, literally.

Give people something to look forward to by bringing in, having delivered, or otherwise supplying *something* edible on a specific day at a specific time each week. Sliced fruit, veggies, or other healthy snacks will also encourage everyone to eat well and get them on the path to feeling better about themselves.

Yes, people will start to look forward to it, and yes, maybe even expect it. If you keep your goal in mind and make a proper recognition moment out of it every time, the weekly treat will be effective *and* yummy.

CARROT ACTION: Don't patronize with candy "prizes." A public recognition moment capped with a healthy treat, however, is a great way to celebrate a team win while providing a needed break. Remember it's not about what you're giving so much as what you say when you give it.

May I Help You?

Just ask.

⌒⌒

Sometimes the easiest and cheapest way to show your gratitude to someone for all of their great work is to offer your help. By asking if there's anything you can to do assist them, you show that you recognize they have a heavy work load and that what they do is critical to the team's success. It also demonstrates your willingness to stay engaged in the mission of the department—even when you find yourself with little to do.

CARROT ACTION: Projects all finished up? Go ask a teammate if he needs anything. Watch your relationship strengthen and your team perform better.

Heating Up the Workplace

Anger makes dull men witty, but it keeps them poor.
—Elizabeth I

The *New York Times* in 2001 asked a large group of employed adults what it feels like to go to work. Respondents described environments in which employees are driven to tears by the bosses (25 percent), are forced to work long hours in order to complete their assignments (52 percent), and some (8 percent) even bemoaned the lousy condition of their chairs. The most disturbing to us was the percentage of people who reported verbal abuse and yelling on the job: 50 percent.

Verbal abuse is simply bad business. It creates an atmosphere that denies openness and communication. It's also a teamwork destroyer, undermining trust. Yelling creates a hierarchy of power that rewards the biggest and loudest at the expense of everyone else.

We're fond of a quotation by Lawrence J. Peter, an educator best known for popularizing the concept of the Peter Principle, "Speak when you are angry—and you will make the best speech you'll ever regret."

CARROT ACTION: If verbal abuse is a fire, there is plenty of kindling near its source. Don't stoke the fire by encouraging others in their anger. The next time a peer starts to complain, acknowledge his or her frustration and lend support without pouring gasoline on the sparks.

Carrot Basics Reminder

Be Specific/Non-vague/Detailed.

Specificity is the foundation/bedrock/basic/gotta have/can't live without/be-all-end-all/first step/square one/all-important/critical/primary characteristic of any and all Carrot actions.

Whether it's a full-scale/no-holds-barred/all systems go/formal/hall-rentin'/tux wearin'/caterer payin'/rip-roarin'/big to-do fiesta/banquet/ceremony/to celebrate the greatest employee that ever walked the Earth/Venus/Mars/Jupiter *or* a simple/no-frills modest/humble, yet meaningful thank-you card, you've got to be specific in expressing the rationale and sentiment of the occasion.

Drilling down and singling out the specific, granular details of a "great job!" is what separates you from the apes/monkeys/primates.

CARROT ACTION: Start with the basics: Send an email message of thanks to a co-worker right now and be as specific as possible about the reason for which you're saying thanks. The website thanks.com has some fun, free emails to use, and best of all you can personalize the messages to the recipient.

It's in the Air

A culture of recognition.

⌒⌒

Great corporate cultures are best built by frequent, specific, and timely recognition. While it's true that other motivators can bring results—fear of getting fired can certainly inspire a burst of energy—lasting advances have to have widespread support.

Business gurus Jack and Suzy Welch point out the connection between engagement and success: "We often ask audiences if they think their companies celebrate success enough, and typically no more than ten percent of the crowd says yes. What a lost opportunity. Celebrating victories along the way is an amazingly effective way to keep people engaged on the whole journey. And we're not talking about celebrating just the big wins."

People are transformed through recognition. Their pride in their company grows. They start to think of themselves differently; they are part of a team of champions. When they see that they are always celebrating, they become accustomed to winning. Even if they are behind on a goal, they find themselves banding together in order to succeed.

CARROT ACTION: Answer the question, "Does my team celebrate success enough?" How can I help us celebrate more?

Is Your Boss Killing You?

Health consequences of workplace distrust.

On a radio program, when we were guests, the host asked his audience: would you rather work for a great boss and get paid minimum wage, or for a miserable, controlling boss who paid you $100 an hour? To our shock, about half of the callers wanted the great boss and much less money. Several mentioned, "It's not worth my health to work for a terrible manager."

This result is obviously unscientific, but there have been recent studies about workers and bad bosses that make the case more convincingly. British scientist George Fieldman conducted research on the role played by employees' perceptions of their bosses and whether interaction styles caused physical health problems.

Depending on whether they liked or disliked their bosses, the participants' diastolic and systolic blood pressure varied in significant degrees. Fieldman concluded that working for a boss they thought unfair could increase employees' risk of coronary heart disease by one-sixth and the risk of stroke by one-third.

Disrespect, it turns out, damages a team, and your health.

CARROT ACTION: Rate your boss. Out of a possible four (with four being the ideal), how many stars would you award him or her? Are there any suggestions you can give your boss (in private) that might help?

Let Me Finish

Don't take the words right out of my mouth.

〜〜

If during your conversations with clients, co-workers, or bosses, you hear them say, "Let me finish," you are probably in trouble.

Often we want to make a point so badly that we don't wait for the other person to finish his sentence before we interrupt, interject, or even shout over others to make our point.

In the rush to get so many things done in our workday we often forget the common courtesy of letting people finish their sentences in simple conversation. It is something that we all see. The problem is when we interrupt our colleagues we have stopped communicating. We are only stating our viewpoints rather than listening to theirs. When this happens, meaningful dialog stops.

Here are simple steps to show respect to those around you and better communicate:

1. Always wait until others are finished talking.
2. Take a breath.
3. Then, answer.

CARROT ACTION: Listen and give the other speaker the respect he or she deserves. It will also give you a chance to think a little longer, and the conversation will flow much better.

Tickets here! Who Needs Two?

Take me out to the ball game.

Baseball. Hockey. Football. Soccer. Ice dancing. One of these is not quite like the others, and yet they all share a certain similarity. You have to pay through the nose to get tickets to go see them. Or do you?

Sometimes tickets will unexpectedly roll your way—maybe from winning them at the state fair prize draw or having a rich uncle who has lifetime Lakers courtside seats. Maybe you're a season ticket holder to a college football team or AAA baseball club.

Next time a pair of ducats to a soccer game or a Dwight Yoakam concert fall into your lap, think about someone in your work group who might enjoy them and give them up as a gesture of gratitude for work well done.

CARROT ACTION: Give away the next set of tickets that come your way as a way to reward a team member for a great job.

Stoolie. Nark. Fink. Tattletale.

Go ahead, rat out your co-workers.

"Nobody likes a tattletale!" your mother warned. It's true that the little busybody who told on you for sleeping through story time was usually the last one chosen for sports and the first one beaten up at recess. But let's turn the idea of a tattletale into something positive. Good tattletales report to the boss all the *great* things their associates are doing.

The fact remains, a manager doesn't have eyes in the back of her head. Or the side for that matter, as that would just be odd. She can only be in one place at a time and typically misses witnessing firsthand all the little (or big) accomplishments of your team.

So, help her out. Tattle in a good way. Pull her aside regularly and rat out your friends. Sing like a lark. Spill the beans. Be a catalyst for ongoing, frequent, and meaningful recognition.

Your mother would be proud.

CARROT ACTION: Stay alert today for opportunities to run to the boss and spill your guts. Just resist the urge to gossip negatively, and keep all your tattling positive.

A Line in the Sand

Make the right decisions before the decision arises.

⌒

Many businesspeople who are dishonored by unethical actions don't necessarily have a long history of deceit. Some simply fall into a trap of greed that escalates into major indiscretions. At some point, after they have proved themselves to their bosses and received responsibility and autonomy, they find themselves in a situation where no one is looking over their shoulders. As the stakes rise, these people falter and begin to take small ethical detours that lead them down a dishonest road.

The people who remain trustworthy throughout their careers decide early that they will never break their personal code of integrity. They will remain true to what they believe is right—despite the allure of money, power, or popularity. In fact, many of the successful people we've talked to use the same phrase: "A line in the sand." People with integrity, they say, draw a line in the sand at some point in their careers and are not willing to cross it, no matter the benefit, no matter the threat.

CARROT ACTION: If you do not lie or cheat on the small things, it is unlikely that you will be corrupted by temptations. Commit to sticking to your internal code of morality.

Canaries

Fear is that little darkroom where negatives are developed.
—Michael Pritchard

To test the danger of a mine, coal miners used to lower a canary that served as an indicator of hazard. If a deadly gas were present, the small bird was affected first—and by "affected" we mean "died"—which sent a warning louder than any siren: get out now!

At your place of employment, you have canaries too. You may even be one of them. The corporate equivalent of the canary is the star employee.

When there's trouble, star employees sense danger, weigh their options, and often they'll be the first to drop—by that we mean leave. It can create a panic that attacks the principal assets of an organization: its people.

It's also a disaster that's preventable. When asked what would have kept them in their job, many high-impact performers say the same thing on the way out the door: "No one ever asked me to stay."

If you're the boss, make sure your canaries (your star employees) know how valued they are. Maybe you're the canary at your job. Don't make the mistake of taking off for the wrong reasons. Ask your boss to define your worth to the team and the organization.

CARROT ACTION: Identify the stars around you and take time today to let them know how much you value them.

Serf-ing USA

A labor statistic you could live without.

Pity the serf! The poor laborers of the Middle Ages had it bad. Bound to feudal manors, they worked the fields for their masters in exchange for protection. These people were considered property. Guess what, though? You're outworking them.

Some 25 million U.S. workers today report working an average of more than fifty hours a week, with 40 percent of those workaholics logging more than sixty hours a week. The average American or Canadian worker puts in a full month of hours (160 to be precise) more each year than a generation ago; more than the citizens of any other Western European country, and even longer hours than medieval peasants did in servitude.

It could be worse. At least we have indoor plumbing. Still, we all have to acknowledge our mutual stress. Let's lighten up on each other.

Be sensitive to the people around you. When their workload gets to be too much, offer a hand.

CARROT ACTION: Identify someone around you who seems to be overwhelmed with work. Make a small difference in their lives by offering temporary assistance.

The Problem of the Lone Ranger

When faced with a tough decision, don't go it alone.

Roman emperor Marcus Aurelius tried once a day to put away his many burdens and create what he called a "space of quiet." The idea is to slow down enough to get a feeling for what your intuitions may be telling you.

Sometimes good people make judgment errors when they don't take enough time to stop and think. It's not a question of morality, they just make a mistake in their rush to a solution. So whenever there's a close call, listen to your inner voice, then seek advice, get a second and third set of eyes and ears.

When seeking advice, choose your advisors carefully, but be willing to discuss the difficult parts of an issue. Talk through the facts, and be forthcoming.

After you've stated all the facts, and collected opinions from your trusted advisors, then it's time again to listen to your own intuition.

CARROT ACTION: Asking for counsel and taking time for reflection are keys to making the right decision. Put yourself in the affected party's shoes to see if you would make a different decision. And, finally, ask if you would want this decision remembered as part of your personal legacy.

Just a Little More

*When asked how much money was enough,
billionaire J. D. Rockefeller smiled and replied,
"Just a little more."*

Reputations are sensitive things. They can be lost in a moment—and take years to rebuild. Unfortunately, this is a reality some businesspeople don't grasp until too late.

There is a good deal of risk associated with making the pursuit of short-term personal gain one's highest and most urgent priority. Look at the track record of companies like Enron, Worldcom, Arthur Andersen, and others. They made a big splash chasing "Just a little more," but were torpedoed by their poor decisions and couldn't stay afloat for the long term.

Trust is the key to long-term business success. Trust is what builds our reputation, and reputations make our careers. After all, we buy from people we trust, we want to work with people we trust, we promote people who are trustworthy. When we make personal integrity our highest priority, the very pursuit of it brings out the best in each of us.

CARROT ACTION: Define integrity for yourself and think about how you would want people to describe your character when you are not in the room.

Don't Go Naked

The power of the trust-filled environment.

In "The Emperor's New Clothes" the emperor commissions unprincipled tailors to sew his robes. Instead of making clothing, they tell him that the robes are of such fine material that only the noblest citizens can see it. Desperate to defend their nobility, his advisors assure him that they could see the robes. And so the emperor wears *nothing at all* in a public procession, and is humiliated.

The moral of the story? The integrity of the people—and the environment—surrounding you is critical. It just may save you from showing up with your (moral) pants down.

Most people who consistently act with integrity do so not just because of who they are, but also because of where they are: They surround themselves with good people and good groups. They have chosen to work someplace positive, cultivate friends and join certain organizations.

The fact is, even a person with almost bulletproof integrity never stops needing the support of trustworthy people in an ethical environment.

CARROT ACTION: Ask yourself, "Am I surrounding myself with trustworthy co-workers and friends? Am I in an ethical environment? If not, what can I do to improve the trust level of my team?"

We *Can* Handle the Truth

When you make a mistake, 'fess up. We can take it.

Becoming a trustworthy person starts with full disclosure—even if the truth is hard to admit. When you are honest, candid, and timely in your communication to your teammates and bosses, and when you tell the truth no matter the consequences, people around you quickly learn they can count on you and that your word means something.

You must have respect for the intelligence and resilience of your co-workers and customers to believe that they can handle the truth, both good and bad. What they cannot accept is dishonesty, breach of integrity, and violations of trust.

And don't forget the flip side to this: When you don't 'fess up, there's a good chance that someone else will be blamed for your mistake. People who protect themselves often cost others, and that almost always comes back twofold.

CARROT ACTION: When was the last time you admitted a mistake to your team? If it's been months or years, you may have a low level of trustworthiness to others.

A-1

The power of believing in yourself

⌒

In 2002, Yang Yang proudly stepped onto the podium and accepted an Olympic gold medal. She was the first Chinese athlete to win a gold medal in an Olympic Winter Games.

We spoke to this speed skater—who won her gold in the women's 500-meter short track—and asked her what she was thinking when they placed the medal around her neck. Her response was profound: "I was thinking, 'When I work hard, I can do anything.'"

Then she got back on the ice and won another gold.

Yang Yang's attitude is exactly right. In her case, there had never been anyone from her country who had won a gold medal in her sport. There was no role model for her success, no benchmark. Her goals pushed her beyond what history said was possible—all in pursuit of recognition.

CARROT ACTION: In your family, there was likely someone who was the first to go to college, the first to accomplish something of great merit. What do you aspire to accomplish that would be a "first"?

What We Really Want

*Education's purpose is to replace
an empty mind with an open one.*
—Malcolm Forbes

For a job well done, we expect something in return. But often in our jobs there's a tight lid on how much compensation is available. Yes, there will be an occasional surprise, but the big bonuses are simply not going to happen for most of us. Not much motivation there, if money is the key motivator at work. The good news is it isn't.

A study by HRM Singapore interviewed three thousand people. When asked, "What do you really want from your job?" employees ranked pay third. Here are the results:

1. Career/learning development opportunities
2. Recognition
3. Pay
4. Relationship with manager

It is our experience that the findings of this study are universal. No one argues that pay is unimportant, but people around the world cite development and recognition as even more important.

CARROT ACTION: Make a list of the top things you want from a job. You might be surprised to discover that once the threshold of good pay is reached, money slides down the list of priorities.

Carrots Basics Reminder

Timely.

Being *timely* in recognizing a co-worker's good deed is one of the three pillars of recognition, along with being frequent and specific.

Sure, you're thinking, timeliness is *good*, but a "pillar"? Come on!

Yes, it is a pillar.

Think it through. When was the last time you called your mother in another time zone to wish her a happy birthday three days after the fact? How well did *that* go over? It's not that you didn't really mean it, but you can bet it was received that way.

Timeliness says, "I care enough about this recognition and about you enough to do it as soon as possible."

CARROT ACTION: If your team pulls together and really scores on a big project, bring in the doughnuts or mete out another kind of award the very next morning.

Need-to-Know

*Many persons have a wrong idea
of what constitutes true happiness.
It is not attained through self-gratification
but through fidelity to a worthy purpose.*
—Helen Keller

We read the comments of a new CEO. The new executive of an energy company introduced himself to his people and stated flatly that regarding communication, he believed in a need-to-know policy. To his mind, giving information to his employees that was outside of their specific job parameters was a distraction and a waste of time.

We winced when we read this. It was clear to us that this was a leader who wanted to control everything. Leaders like this are dinosaurs today. Communication is simply too easy to come by. It's like water in your hand: it's going to find a way out no matter how tightly you make a fist.

Why would any leader restrict his team from ideas and therefore keep them from coming up with new and better ones? We guessed the CEO would last a year. We were wrong. It was less.

CARROT ACTION: Stand up and ask questions of those around you. As new challenges arise, join in the conversation about how you can help.

Snow Removal

It's the little (cold) things.

⌒⌒

If you live in a snowless clime, we admire (and resent) you. Congratulations on making it into work today, by the way, after what was probably a four-hour commute on a three-mile stretch of highway. Warmth comes at a cost.

But we digress.

If you don't, this winter remember to bring a warm pair of gloves, a shovel, and snow scraper to work each day (leave them in your car, of course). On a snowy day, to show appreciation for a co-worker's help on a project, coming up with an innovative idea, or any other praiseworthy accomplishment, sneak out to their car and scrape off and clean all their windows. Shovel away a clear path for them to get to the car door.

CARROT ACTION: Put the gear in your car tonight, so you can be ready tomorrow, just in case.

Cheese Power

What's your flavor?

This is going to sound like a stretch (although some cheeses do stretch). Cheese is much like communication. There are countless varieties and uses. It's different depending on how it's applied and to what it's applied. And, most people prefer some types of communication over others.

Realize that serving up effective communication is much like serving up a tray of cheeses. Watch how people around you respond to each flavor. Watch how they apply it, and start creating a menu for the future—so you know exactly what type of communication will satisfy.

CARROT ACTION: Conduct your own communication taste test to truly understand your own favorites—which type of communication intrigues you the most, turns you off, turns you on, and generates the biggest response.

That's Rich

Big accomplishment—big reward.

Imagine winning an award like Maria Grimaldi did at Rich Products Corporation in Buffalo: her team and their spouses were given the corporate jet for a five-day vacation anywhere they wanted to go in the world . . . and they chose Rochester.

Not really. But seriously, the award was given to the team that had moved a newly acquired company to a new spot, meshed processes and systems into Rich's, and boosted sales—all while making the move transparent to customers. Even more impressive, the team delivered the project early and under budget, thereby adding millions of dollars to Rich's bottom line. Not bad.

"The prize is absolutely surreal," Grimaldi said. "But even without that, I've been surprised how much the recognition has meant to me." The award, after all, was a result of a nomination by her peers at the corporation. "I feel a need to live worthy of the recognition I've earned. I feel driven to consistently display the kind of work ethic I'm capable of, do the right thing, and go the extra mile."

CARROT ACTION: Awards have short-term and long-term benefits. When you are given recognition, how does that affect your motivation afterward?

It's Catchy

The spread of problems and solutions.

Have you ever thought about how quickly a virus spreads? Happily, the same principal that applies to infection also applies to positive ideas and solutions to problems.

When someone is praised for his work, a positive virus is spread. People who witness recognition are infected. They want to experience it too.

KPMG implemented a national recognition program, called Encore. "Recognition has become a fever," said Sylvia Brandes, director of compensation for KPMG's 19,000 U.S. employees. "What we found is that groups that do not present a lot of Encores [awards] in their organization tend to have greater turnover. We also found turnover among people who received an award was half that of those who hadn't received an award. And we found a correlation between functions or organizations that had higher scores for recognition and the number of Encore awards that were given within that group."

CARROT ACTION: If you had to name three people in your organization that "infect" you in a positive way, who would they be and why? Tell them that you appreciate their energy.

Winning at Any Cost

It's an idea that's not only wrong, but dangerous.

⌒⌒

What's the single biggest reason most people won't admit a mistake? They think they are going to be punished. So, the next time someone around you admits he's messed up, don't look down on him, but laud him in front of others and thank him for his honesty.

Open communication and full disclosure are among the most difficult lessons we must learn as businesspeople, but many of us will go through our entire careers without developing these skills. And that keeps us from attaining greatness.

The first step is developing a willingness to be wrong when you make a mistake. We're not suggesting you admit failure daily, but sometimes. As soon as you say "I blew it," everyone else on your team knows it's also okay to make a mistake now and then. And that creates an environment where innovation and trust can thrive.

What others won't forgive is a lack of disclosure, leaving out certain parts of the story, or distorting facts to make your side look better.

CARROT ACTION: Share *all* pertinent information with your co-workers, not just that which will help make your case. When you make a mistake, acknowledge failure, apologize, and make amends.

Corkboard

Board of Fame.

Set up a bulletin board in your department for the world (other departments or passersby) to see. Post on it every thank-you card or printouts of positive feedback emails you receive from internal or external customers. Any correspondence, snail mail or email, or any clipping from a newspaper or from a blog that mentions your co-worker's name or gives him or her any due respect totally qualifies.

It's a simple, but meaningful way to show team pride and throw a little Carrot "props" to a deserving associate.

CARROT ACTION: Be the first to post something positive about someone on your team.

Getting in Line

*Is it possible to merge your goals and the goals
of the organization?*

When your boss says, "good job," what does she mean,
exactly?

Not to detract from the compliment, but it's important
that your "good job" be tied to the goals of the organization. You want to be liked by leadership, sure, but the
achievement that will bring you lasting recognition and
advancement is found in a single word: alignment.

When your goals and the goals of the organization are
aligned, everyone benefits mutually. The organization has
a mission, vision, and values. When these can become *your*
mission, vision, and values, as well, each act on your part
furthers the organization. It's a simple concept, but it is
counter to the prevailing attitude of "working for the man."
Rather, you are working with each other for mutual success.
Then, when your boss says, "good job," she is really saying, "You are important to us, you are engaged in the right
activities, you deserve recognition."

CARROT ACTION: Test yourself: What are the mission, vision,
and values of the organization where you work? Can you
name them? How can you make your work align with those
concepts?

Roses Are Red . . .

Send a dozen today.

Business aside, when is the last time you recognized the most important people in your life—your family, friends, or other loved ones at home?

Don't miss this chance to tell the people closest to you that you love them. No one can hear it enough and it never gets old.

CARROT ACTION: This Valentine's Day, instead of just giving roses, include a love note, expressing specifically why you love that person so much. It will make whoever gets the roses feel great—and you won't feel so bad yourself.

Skirting the Pink Slip

Five tips to keep your job in scary times.

In troubling times, people are worried about keeping their jobs, and for good reason. You've heard the saying, a rising tide raises all boats? The opposite also feels true. As the waters recede, every boat, no matter how large and powerful, worries about getting left high and dry on the shoals.

So, what can you do to avoid getting the pink slip?

- Remind your boss that you are close to the money. Be a rainmaker.
- Recommunicate your goals. Your boss needs to know that you are forward-thinking, and have a plan to accomplish your goals.
- Be the team member who is optimistic, and confident.
- Be trusted, and visible. It's important to remember that you can't build trust by hiding in your cubicle.
- Recognize yourself and others. Let go of the "me" attitude.

CARROT ACTION: **What not to do:** Don't allow your anxiety to turn into a cycle of cynicism and a sense of inevitable doom. If there ever was a time to show what you can bring to the table, it's now.

Missing in Action

The hidden costs of employees who don't give their all.

⌣

Imagine that you're on a rowing team, but only half the oars are in the water. Unfortunately, this happens in business all the time.

Unlike the problem of absenteeism, in the case of what's called presenteeism, the chairs are full, but some of the people aren't working.

Presenteeism, according to *The Harvard Business Review*, costs American companies $150 billion each year. It's likely a problem for your team and company, too. To team members, it means that less gets accomplished, less efficiently than it should. It takes more energy to motivate the slackers, and others have to pick up the slack.

What's wrong with these no-shows who show up anyway? Perhaps they're focused on problems at home or office gossip; they're burned out, stressed, or underused. But their problems are your problems. Therefore, it's in your best interest to get these people motivated with clear goals and positive accountability.

CARROT ACTION: Presenteeism is a malady surrounded by enablers. When someone isn't pulling his or her weight in your organization, point out the problem honestly in a way that encourages everyone to actively pursue common goals. Have the person develop a plan to get back on track. Their ownership is critical to their success.

Games People Play

Is business a poker game where bluffing is allowed?

We've spent a lot of time thinking about the gray areas in business, and why people bend or break the rules. We are intrigued by gut-wrenching, sleepless-night decisions we make as businesspeople. After all, a lot of business is "played" in the gray realm.

Some ethicists believe there are times when games are played in business. For instance, you may announce that you will build a plant in one city because you want a competitor to think so, but you are really going to build it in another state entirely. These ethicists thus see business as a poker game, where people bluff when they need to.

However, many of the leaders we talked to do not share this belief. After all, how would customers and potential business partners judge the bending of the rules in the above example? Would they believe the individuals involved were straight shooters if, through a merger or other alliance, they were to do business with those same competitors at a later date? Would they think twice?

CARROT ACTION: Shady gamesmanship is rarely acceptable. Find ways to do business without violating your individual or company core principles.

Take a Break

Fresh air for fresh ideas.

Gather up as many associates who will go and take a ten-minute walk outside twice a day. It's the same amount of time they would take if they were smokers. The walk will reinvigorate you and your co-workers physically and give you a few minutes to chat. You'd be surprised at some of the things you might be inspired to discuss.

Walk next to and talk to someone other than your standard go-to friend. Make an attempt to get to know the others on your team. Ask about their family or talk about the movie you saw over the weekend.

CARROT ACTION: Encourage and invite co-workers to head outside this very afternoon.

Great Recognition Ideas: Goal Setting

The big secret in life is that there is no big secret.
Whatever your goal, you can get there
if you're willing to work.
—Oprah Winfrey

Here are three specific ideas on goal setting when it comes to employee recognition.

Knowledge is power when it comes to recognition, but you have to know the people you will recognize. Make a goal to find out one new item about each person you work with every day.

Variety is the spice of life. If you make assignments, then give employees crucial tasks that stretch their skills and are separate from their job descriptions. Provide training, backup resources, and personnel necessary for success.

To help you remember to acknowledge others, place three coins in your right pocket at the beginning of each day. As you reward successful behavior during the day, transfer a coin to your left pocket. At the end of the day, all three coins should have migrated.

CARROT ACTION: Nourish an atmosphere of goal setting by creating personal goals and displaying them in view of others.

Public Wisdumb

*Smoking kills. If you're killed,
you've lost a very important part of your life.*
—Brooke Shields

For many of us, public speaking is one of the most frightening activities in the world. Yet, many times in business, we're asked to share something publicly—with a real audience who is actually listening to what we say.

When it's your turn to speak publicly, here are a few tips to overcome the jitters and effectively communicate your message.

- Don't memorize, just practice. You're the content expert, telling people about what you know best. You're not reciting Shakespeare.
- Get away from the podium. Podiums hide people instead of spotlighting them—creating a situation where you speak at people not with them.
- Pause between thoughts. It shows you're thinking.
- If all else fails, tell a joke, even a corny or self-effacing one.

CARROT ACTION: To practice speaking publicly call your team together just to share status updates on projects. Ask everyone in the circle to share. Even these small steps help people get more comfortable in front of a crowd.

Snail Mail

Go through the post.

Though you sit only feet away from each other and you work closely nine hours a day and may even sit by each other at lunch, consider handwriting a sincere thank you letter to your workmate and dropping it in the post to their home. There's still nothing as exciting as receiving an actual letter in the mail, now more than ever, as the practice is all but extinct.

The stamp, the postmark, and the sealed envelope (especially one without a little plastic window, i.e., a bill) combine to create a nice experience for the recipient. Make sure you write legibly and follow the Carrot Principle of *specifically* pointing out the reasons for the appreciation.

CARROT ACTION: Buy some actual stationery; they still sell it. Do not grab a sheet of paper off the printer. Start crafting a handwritten letter today.

Battle Cries

The greatness of Washington.

On December 31, 1776, the American revolutionary army was preparing to go home. For all intents and purposes the war was over, and they had lost. On this difficult day, George Washington spoke to the troops, and appealed to their practicality and their pocket books. He offered the men a $10 bonus. All declined.

Then Washington made one last attempt. This time the plea was different. He spoke to them with great affection. He praised them for their sacrifice and their courage. He acknowledged that they had done more and given more than anyone could have ever expected. He asked them to think about their freedom and their families. To think about what they, and only they, could do. If they would stay and fight with him for just three more months, they could change the world! He appealed to the greater good, not just the short-term money in hand.

This time when the drums rolled, they all stepped forward.

Washington learned that people would do more for a great cause than they will for cash.

CARROT ACTION: In a crisis, become a leader of your teammates. Ask them, how will you look upon this moment ten years from now?

Fun and Games

Bowling for laughs.

The beauty of bowling is that it's easy to play, even if you're bad at it. Beyond that, it's a slow moving game that gives you a chance to sit and laugh and talk. One department of workers we know has found that most alleys have a grill with decent lunch specials.

Getting five or ten people together to go eat lunch and knock down some pins is a great way to celebrate a team victory, a completed project, or someone's work anniversary.

CARROT ACTION: Take thirty seconds and Google "bowling" in your area. See if the alley serves lunch, and, if so, schedule a Friday when most of your team can go.

No More Mondays

No more "next weeks." No more excuses.

There are readers at this very second (you know who you are) who plan to start exercising, start dieting, and stop smoking . . . on Monday. There are also readers who have an intimidating file folder—sitting right up there at the corner of the desk—that will be opened next Monday.

Supposedly a day for fresh starts, Mondays have become a chronic crutch. They're the day in which we schedule everything we don't want to do—the day that we know will be miserable.

What if we started a diet on Friday? What if we dove into the dreaded projects on Friday morning? Maybe the fact that we started would actually make the weekend more exciting.

CARROT ACTION: Open that file or start that project you've been putting off first thing this Friday.

Great Recognition Ideas: Communication

*Think like a wise man but communicate
in the language of the people.*
—William Butler Yeats

In many ways, recognition has at its core a need to communicate excellence to others. Yes, it's a set of golf clubs at the retirement party, but recognition is also the small, ongoing practice of telling people they matter to you. So, try the following:

1. Before the end of each day, jot down three things that went well. This is good for your work, home, and social life. This exercise provides a continuous reservoir of recognition possibilities.
2. A manager can't be everywhere at once. Buy a stack of thank you cards. As you see co-workers' excellence, recognize their achievements.

Fewer than half of managers attempt to recognize the work of their people. Thus, if you are part of a recognition culture, you will have a strategic advantage over your peers and competitors.

CARROT ACTION: The biggest mistake people make is to assume those around them don't need to hear words of praise. Let honest appreciation come out, with specific ways they've helped you or the team.

More Than Words

Let there be few words and many deeds,
and may they be done well.
—St. Vincent Pallotti

In trying times, communication is best applied through action.

Legends are passed on through history books—stories of great men and women rising to the aid of others. Today, when people, groups, or companies perform great deeds, press releases are broadcast out to media organizations. Yet sometimes the greatest deeds are those that are never talked about—because words simply might undermine the ultimate message or goal.

Recently, as the world faced an economic downturn, at least a few people or organizations understood a core message that needed to be communicated. The Associated Press revealed that at least nine American universities received donations of well over $1 million each from anonymous donors—a message of hope for the future. Those donations ranged in size from $1.5 million for the University of North Carolina–Asheville to $8 million for Purdue University in Indiana.

In these cases, though the donors' identities are unknown, the message of altruistic giving was loud and clear.

CARROT ACTION: Commit a secret good deed today. The only person that needs to know about your actions is you.

Steer Clear

Keep away from the edge.

A wealthy man who was looking to hire a personal driver presented each candidate with the following scenario. "Imagine you are driving me to an engagement. We are late. The shortest route includes a dangerous stretch of road through a winding canyon with a thousand-foot cliff on the shoulder. I offer you $1,000 if we arrive on time. Traveling at seventy miles per hour, how close could you get to the edge?" The first candidate thought for a moment and then replied, "twelve inches." The second answered, "six inches." The third candidate said, "I'd stay as far away from the edge of the cliff as possible."

The third guy got the job.

Likewise, a trustworthy person stays far away from situations where she could be tempted by that which might corrupt her.

Each decision you make sends subtle hints about your character. Not only can bad decisions based on short-term thinking taint your reputation, but also that of the entire organization.

CARROT ACTION: We are all human and can make mistakes, so consider a few business temptations you might face. Decide today to steer clear of them.

Give Credit Where It's Due

Glory—enough and to spare.

⌒⌒

At work or at home, a true altruist is a rare and extremely valued asset. Being generous, selfless, and benevolent are qualities spoken of in the highest terms but too infrequently witnessed. For example, when co-workers are singled out for excellent work or a great idea, many of us clap our hands and pat their backs, but inside we feel a sense of panic or anxiety.

"Oh no," we worry, "that's less glory and praise for *me*, now."

At the very core of a happy, high-functioning team is giving credit where credit is due . . . and doing it with a generous, jealousy-free heart. Even if, because of poor management or an oversight, you believe *you* should have been recognized as well.

CARROT ACTION: Credit and praise are not like the "matter" you learned about in science class; there is *not* a finite amount of either. We won't run out of it. You'll eventually get yours. So keep giving.

Assets

Focus first on the human kind.

The competition is fierce. Companies are forced to gain market share. The pressure to innovate, integrate, and implement is intense. Employees are battling internally and externally for position—securing themselves a spot in the future of success. They're honing their skill and mastering their crafts. They're throwing themselves vigorously into continued education, leadership development, management training, and trade classes. And, when they accomplish greatness they'll be the leaders—unbreakable, unstoppable, and equipped for anything. Right?

If you had asked celebrities Michael J. Fox, Lance Armstrong, or the late Christopher Reeves how their focus changed—the primary focus being simply surviving not in the rat race but as part of the human race—they would tell you to not forget to take care of the human element—you.

CARROT ACTION: Healthy humans are productive humans. And that means emotional health, a positive attitude, expressing appreciation, accepting others, and taking care of yourself. Take care of yourself today. It's a basic human need.

Attitude Survey Part 1

Engagement.

Thomas Jefferson said, "Determine never to be idle . . . It is wonderful how much may be done if we are always doing." And, in fact, the third president of the United States was the poster child for a lifetime of activity. Aside from his roles in government, he was also a farmer, architect, archaeologist, paleontologist, inventor, author, and founder of a university.

Take the following test. This is a survey that measures engagement and satisfaction. We'll divide it into two parts. The first: engagement; the second: satisfaction. For the engagement survey, respond to the following statements:

- Employees in my department consistently put in extra effort beyond what is expected.
- Employees in my department are highly motivated to contribute to the success of the organization.
- Employees in my department consistently look for more efficient and effective ways of getting the job done.

CARROT ACTION: Tally your responses and give yourself a letter grade on each question to reflect how your department (and yourself) rate in terms of engagement.

Attitude Survey Part 1A

More engagement questions.

Today we will conduct the second part of the engagement survey.

Respond to the following statements:

* Employees in my department have a strong sense of personal accomplishment in their work.
* Employees in my department understand how their roles help the organization meet its goals.
* Employees in my department always have a positive attitude when performing their duties at work.
* My manager does a good job of recognizing employee contributions.

CARROT ACTION: Look back over the seven engagement questions from the past two days (they were placed in order of importance) and tally your total responses. Give yourself a final letter grade to reflect how your department (and yourself) rate, in terms of engagement. If you scored poorly, begin to improve conditions today.

Attitude Survey Part 2

Satisfaction.

Sir Winston Churchill made a statement about progress that we think has great value: "Every day you may make progress. Every step may be fruitful. Yet there will stretch out before you an ever-lengthening, ever-ascending, ever-improving path. You know you will never get to the end of the journey. But this, so far from discouraging, only adds to the joy and glory of the climb."

Today, we move on to the second part of our survey. Your responses to these statements will measure satisfaction.

- At work, I have the opportunity to do what I do best every day.
- My performance is evaluated in a manner that makes me feel positive about working.
- Conflicts are managed in a way that results in positive solutions.
- My opinions seem to matter to my manager.
- My manager shares all the information my co-workers and I need in order to feel part of the team.

CARROT ACTION: Tally your responses, again using a letter grade to reflect your level of satisfaction with each question.

Attitude Survey Part 2A

More satisfaction.

Today you'll take the last part of our survey. Here are more statements about satisfaction:

- I receive the information I need to do my job.
- The organization has developed work/life policies that address my needs.
- I trust my immediate manager.
- During the past year, communication between leadership and employees has improved.
- My manager does a good job of recognizing employee contributions.
- I have recently received praise for my work.

A risk in taking a test like this is that it may reveal just how unhappy you are in your workplace. Don't allow these sentiments to overwhelm you. These questions are slanted toward the ideal, and while some work environments concentrate on employee satisfaction, not all companies have it figured out . . . yet.

Think of how you can grow in the right direction.

CARROT ACTION: Tally your responses and give yourself an overall letter grade to reflect your level of satisfaction. If you are falling short, think about how you can improve your morale. A good way to start might be to help others raise their satisfaction levels.

Walls

Unnatural divisions.

Do you know the Robert Frost poem, "Mending Wall"? In it, Frost describes an old stone wall that divides his property from his neighbor. One spring day, the two men walk along the wall and they replace fallen stones.

Frost wonders why they have a wall in the first place. Ultimately, Frost repairs the wall against his better judgment, if only to keep the peace. In the final line of the poem, his neighbor justifies the work by quoting a family mantra, "Good fences make good neighbors."

In business there are internal walls that management builds between itself and line employees. Communication between the two can become formal and limited. The problem with corporate walls is that they are by their nature divisive and fracturing.

Walls can be replaced by trust and communication, and that helps management to engage their work neighbors in supportive and encouraging ways.

CARROT ACTION: On occasions when leadership and employees are together, maximize those moments by engaging leadership on a personal level. Introduce yourself, extend your hand. Don't allow yourself to be intimidated by the walls of formality.

Doughnuts

Even skinny people like doughnuts

Want to recognize your team? Two dozen Krispy Kreme originals.

Boom.

Nuff said.

CARROT ACTION: Prepare yourself by not eating for seventy-two hours beforehand.

Talk the Talk

Bad corporate behavior.

Companies like to present themselves as open, communicative places. But the truth is sometimes the opposite. Just as a business will hang a suggestion box and then never look inside, organizations have adopted the talk of openness in their vision statements and outward comments to employees or the public without actually becoming open.

Positive, lasting change in this regard always filters from the top down, but you have an important role to play. When your organization initiates a program that encourages communication, take it seriously and do your part.

CARROT ACTION: You have nothing to lose by walking the walk and talking the talk. Give new communication initiatives a chance by providing suggestions when asked, giving honest feedback, and contributing to new projects.

Most Excellent

*The ancient Greek definition of happiness was
the full use of your powers along lines of excellence.*
—*John F. Kennedy*

"My manager recognizes excellence." How would you respond to the that statement?

A survey conducted for us by HealthStream Research asked the question and discovered a rock-solid correlation between managers' skills at recognition and the perception by their employees that they were effective leaders. The study showed that when respondents rated managers highly in recognition skills, the managers also rated extremely high in what we call leadership's Basic Four skills (goal setting, open communication, building trust, and accountability).

Specifically, when an employee states that a manager is effective at praise, she will almost always say, "I trust my manager," as well. These results strongly suggest that a significant predictor of a leader's management skills (the Basic Four) is his or her ability to recognize excellence. The bottom line is simple: great management begins when recognition is added to the main characteristics of leadership.

CARROT ACTION: Compare managers in your work history. For each of them, respond to the question, "My manager recognizes excellence." Was there a correlation between their ability to recognize excellence and their leadership effectiveness?

Mistaakes Happan

Be not ashamed of mistakes and thus make them crimes.
—Confucius

An employee once said to us, "When I make a mistake I'm recognized 100 percent of the time; when I do something great, I'm *not* recognized 99 percent of the time."

At CACI, a leading information technology firm headquartered in Arlington, Virginia, employees benefit from a cadre of impressive recognition programs designed to acknowledge great work. And yet CACI also wants to address errors, but in a way that is productive. The retired CEO Dr. J. P. London told us: "At CACI, we hold ourselves accountable for being honest in all our dealings. We don't make excuses; we make it RIGHT. Of course, that doesn't mean that we never make mistakes. Every organization does. And we are no different. We know we are not perfect, and we take ownership when we are in error. (After all, if you can't admit a mistake, you certainly can't fix it.) Then we correct our mistakes, and we correct them quickly. We do this even when it hurts." Wise words, indeed.

CARROT ACTION: Consider if the experience of your last error (and its aftermath) made you more likely or less likely to speak up quickly the next time a mistake occurs? If your experience was negative, it's time to bring your group together to talk about how to have more open and honest discussions.

Email

Not all unsolicited messages are SPAM.

Amid the barrage of unsolicited emails, isn't it refreshing to see a subject line that *doesn't* include the phrases "natural enhancement" or "I am a Saudi Arabian billionaire"?

Sending a simple "thank you" message via email is less impactful than writing it out by hand or saying it face to face, but don't underestimate the value of typing. "Thanks so much" or "You're the best" in an email subject line cuts through the endless headers and stands out as a "must read."

In the body of your email remember to be specific in your thanks or praise. Sometimes you may want to "cc" other personnel who may benefit from reading about the recipient's actions.

CARROT ACTION: Send an email of praise or thanks to someone right now. Copy the world and count how many additional people add their kudos.

What's Your Word Worth?

Is your promise worth its weight in gold?

Not too long ago in business, when you gave your word, it was worth something.

Today, you'll starve waiting for someone who said, "Let's do lunch," to actually take you out for a meal. "I love you" can mean anything from a profound attachment to simple gratitude, as in, "I love you! Thanks for getting me that file!"

Of course, these are lighthearted illustrations of a real problem in business: There simply aren't enough people out there who you can trust. And, simply put, people don't stay long in teams devoid of trust. Management researchers James Kouzes and Barry Posner call trust "the most significant predictor of individual satisfaction within (an) organization."

All of us are trying to build stronger relationships in business—with our co-workers, customers, bosses, and other associates. Great businesspeople do what they say they'll do, and that makes all the difference in relationship building.

CARROT ACTION: Think of the promises you've made lately. Know that trusted people move heaven and earth to live up to them, and do the same.

Carrots for Life

*They might push them off their plates,
but kids LOVE carrots.*

⌒⌐

Now that you're becoming a master Carrot wielder at work (careful, the pointy end can put an eye out!), it's time to bring your game home. If you have children living with you, be sure to extend the same Carrot courtesies with them that you do with your workmates.

Remember to be specific in your praise and appreciation and you'll see the dividends. Imagine:

> *You*: I love the way you made your bed today, Ralphie. You pulled it tight and there are no wrinkles. Wow, really well done!
>
> *Ralphie*: Who *are* you, and what have you done with Mommy/Daddy!?

Seriously, though, with that kind of specific recognition Ralphie will not only be more likely to make his bed but will probably look for other things to clean up just to hear your specific praise.

CARROT ACTION: Say something *positive* and *specific* to each of your children today—no negatives for the whole day.

Great Recognition Ideas: Trust

It is better to suffer wrong than to do it,
and happier to be sometimes cheated than not to trust.
—Samuel Johnson

A curious thing about trust: it is the by-product of action. Here are three great trust actions.

1. Be an active listener. Make eye contact. Take notes. Ask questions. When you demonstrate that you are truly engaged, people will open up to you and trust you.

2. When someone makes a mistake in an attempt to move into new territory, reward it. Acknowledge the courage involved in taking the risk rather than concentrating on the negative. Innovation requires trial and error.

3. When money is tight, organizations consider cutting back on recognition. Don't do it. In tough times, people need the motivation and energy that recognition brings. They will trust their leaders more and give their all to turn things around.

CARROT ACTION: Today, stop acting like you deserve others' trust, act like you are trying to earn it. Remember that most people are skeptical. We like to keep in mind the positive thinking of Henry L. Stimson, former U.S. Secretary of State, "The only way to make a man trustworthy is to trust him."

Out in the Open

Privacy vs. public recognition.

It's time for your recognition. Would you prefer to receive praise (a) in private; (b) in front of the entire organization; (c) with your team only, or (d) in a dimly lit mine shaft?

There's no single right way to praise someone. In the United States, the majority of people prefer team recognition. The same is true in Mexico, Singapore, and Brazil. But in Russia, Japan, and German, the majority of employees prefer private recognition with just the boss. Can you guess which countries have a majority of employees who prefer to receive praise in front of the entire organization? China and India.

Our cultures affect how we like to be recognized, but our individual personalities also influence our decisions about public versus private praise.

It should be up to you to determine how you are recognized. The last thing the corporation wants to do is to embarrass their star employee. Still, you never know: someone who is a bit shy might discover that having people acknowledging his or her hard work is a pretty great feeling.

CARROT ACTION: When you are selected for recognition, communicate with leadership about the forum in which you feel most comfortable to receive the honor. On the flip side, if you are a leader, ask.

Showing Recognition

You can't wait for inspiration.
You have to go after it with a club.
—Jack London

It's a skill to be able to convey recognition in ways that are meaningful and memorable. It requires creativity and inspiration. And practice. There is a learning curve that should begin with everyone, not just managers. Here are two ideas to get you thinking about possibilities for formal and informal recognition moments.

There's a tug of war between work and home responsibilities. You feel it, and so do your team members. The next time one of them merits an award, honor her family's contribution too: send a basket of food to her significant other with a note thanking him for his sacrifice.

When a leader is away, recognition can (and should) still occur. Managers can prepay for a lunch or have the cafeteria deliver drinks and doughnuts to that employee who deserves extra attention. And what about that empty prime parking spot?

CARROT ACTION: Recognition comes down to this: what kind of person do you want to be? Acts of recognition large and small are the gateway to a generous reputation.

Don't Cut Corners

The erosion of trust is rarely spectacular, but gradual.

The slippery slope that some businesspeople slide down is rarely as quick as in a Hollywood blockbuster (think *Ernest Goes to Camp*). It usually occurs as a slipping of standards.

Most companies start out by expecting their people to measure up to rigorous standards, but when people who cut corners start being acclaimed for it, others begin to feel that if they aren't cutting corners they aren't doing the right thing for their companies, or that they will be left behind.

The right goal is to run your business life in a way that builds long-term value for shareholders, co-workers, and customers. The fraud that happens in corporations on a large scale often starts out on a small scale. People justify wrongdoing by thinking that the company owes them. Thus, fraudulent behavior becomes easier to justify.

A CEO once told us "little things count. We teach employees that we never lie. Like when someone calls in to talk to a manager and their assistant says they are in a meeting, when they are not. It's the little things that your employees notice."

CARROT ACTION: Taking the high road on seemingly trivial decisions is easy, and sets you up for success with bigger decisions. Be careful with expense reimbursements, time sheets, and other small ways people can start slipping.

What Do You Value?

*Forty-five percent of employees have nothing
of value from their company.*

In sports, championship rings are a symbol of excellence. We are friends with a coach who proudly wears a Stanley Cup championship ring, which symbolizes his team's supremacy in the 2003 National Hockey League playoffs. The team logo is prominently displayed in precious gems, and the man's pride in that symbol is worth much more than the cost of the ring.

That ring is a constant reminder of the players he coached and the hard work of that season. He will treasure the ring for a lifetime, and his children wouldn't think of selling it on eBay after he's gone. It will be an heirloom for generations.

We recently surveyed ten thousand employees and found that almost half responded "no" when asked, "Do you own anything of value with the corporate symbol?" What a missed opportunity. Those of us who care about our organizations have an inherent sense of pride in the symbol of that firm.

CARROT ACTION: Create an award for your team that contains the corporate symbol. Make earning the award challenging, and the presentation a meaningful event.

The Early Bird Gets Skinny

Let's get physical, physical.

⌒

We've all told ourselves the same thing: If I only had an extra half hour a day I could lose this butt/gut. But time is precious before and after work to get the lawn mowed, dine with the loved ones, catch a ball game, or attend civic or church activities. And *Wipeout* isn't going to watch itself, now is it?

So, what's the answer?

For the sake of your own health, a happier home life, and a more productive career, get up thirty minutes earlier than normal two or three times a week to allow time for a walk, jog, or swim. Get together with others at work and hold each other accountable by setting team goals for weight loss, body fat percentages, or just time spent working out.

CARROT ACTION: Set exercise goals specific to your needs. Share them with others and encourage them to set goals as well. Begin tomorrow morning. No excuses.

The Fine Print

*Trust men and they will be true to you; treat them greatly,
and they will show themselves great.*
—Ralph Waldo Emerson

According to the Oxford English Dictionary, the word "reciprocity" has two meanings, both of which apply to your business life.

The first meaning describes a mutual action that includes a give and take by both parties. Correspondence is an example.

The second meaning is especially interesting because it requires that both parties concede something for mutual benefit. By their concession, the two parties establish a relationship that is binding. Treaties are an example.

The late Harvard Business School professor Louis Barnes applied reciprocity to trust. At a most basic level, he said, people respond in kind to the way they are treated.

Inside an organization, trust can't occur without participation from everyone. Managers have to listen and respect employees, and vice versa. They have to worry more about the success of the team, because great teams will make them successful.

CARROT ACTION: People tend to think of themselves in flattering terms. But the virtue of being trustworthy is subjective. Be honest with yourself: Are you someone people trust? Ask people you know who will give you honest feedback.

Stop the Presses

Get your people in the newsletter.

Have an employee's picture included in the employee newsletter, and highlight the great work he's been doing. Most smart newsletter editors are looking for this kind of information, especially if it highlights innovation, customer service, or another great win for the organization.

CARROT ACTION: When it's printed, have the article framed and signed with thanks from the team. This is a great keepsake and a terrific reward.

Don't Wait Until They Leave

Tell others how much they matter—today.

When Chester's oldest son finished a summer job at a retailer, he shared an insight. He said it was fun to receive a paycheck, to work the register, and to work with his co-workers, but when he came home from his last day, he had a more significant revelation.

He said, "Dad I wish every day at work was my last day."

Why?

"Because on my last day they told me how much they liked me working there."

How often do we wait until their last day to tell people we work with how much they have meant to our team and our business? What a shame.

In a Carrot Culture there should be a little recognition every day—at least every week. The last day is too late.

CARROT ACTION: Don't wait until a co-worker's last day to say thank you. If you think someone valuable is on her way out, or if you just think she is valuable, tell her today how much she means to you and the team.

The Prize Closet

Yeah! Free stuff.

Remember the gold star we got in school. There wasn't much some people wouldn't do for that simple acknowledgment.

Sometimes getting even the simplest little treat or gift from a co-worker or boss is enough to give us the extra energy to finish out the day with panache. When something is proffered for free, it excites us even if its hard value is next to zero.

CARROT ACTION: People go crazy for little tchotchkes from trade shows or conventions, so next time you're sent to Orlando for the Annual Show of Well Intentioned Personnel Executives (ASWIPE), grab a few little freebies here and there and shower them on your co-workers. It's your way of saying, "I was thinking of you guys back here working while I was on Splash Mountain."

Great Recognition Ideas: Accountability

We have too many high sounding words,
and too few actions that correspond with them.
—Abigail Adams

We love to talk about accountability because ultimately it boils down to fairness. Many corporations simply don't understand the need to acknowledge the good work people accomplish. Here are three great ideas.

Dependability is an underrated virtue. You probably know someone near you who always comes through, meets deadlines, and does solid work, but is rarely acknowledged. Fix that.

When a customer or co-worker compliments someone on your team, take notes. Get the details and record them in a file that can be shared during the employee's review.

Promote people publicly. When a team member is promoted, gather the group together and celebrate the success of the individual. Be sure to relate the behaviors that caused the employee to be promoted, and express appreciation at the same time.

CARROT ACTION: The phrase "holding someone accountable" has a negative connotation. Encourage others to think of accountability more positively. When someone is accountable, he or she owns responsibility and is eager to accomplish goals.

Gain Some Respect

The relationship of respect and trust.

One synonym of trust is to have respect. In other words, you can't go wrong by wanting and working to become more trustworthy; people who do come out more respected and successful in business and in life.

It is an enormously valuable asset when people say about their salesperson, employee, spouse, parent, doctor, friend, mechanic, or teammate: "You can trust him and his word."

The bottom line is that ethical behavior should be a route to gaining the trust and respect of people for whom you are responsible. That bears repeating. We act with integrity so that we can gain the trust of those for whom we are responsible. And there are many: our teammates, our families, our friends, our employers, our customers.

CARROT ACTION: Employees don't follow leaders they don't trust, employers don't hire or promote people they don't trust, clients don't buy from suppliers they distrust. The best way to become trustworthy is to do what you say you will do, even if you have to move heaven and earth to make it happen.

On the First Day

New on the job.

⌒

Have you heard the one about the guy who died and went to the pearly gates? Upon his arrival, St. Peter tells him he gets to choose where to spend eternity: heaven or hell. "But first," Peter says, "You have to spend a day in both places."

He decides to check out heaven first. It's very nice, of course, fluffy white seating, harp music, lots of robes. Next day, hell. The guy thinks, how bad can it be? I can last one day.

So he's surprised when he gets there to find himself in the hippest place, eating delicious food, and talking to fascinating people. At the end of the day, he's had such a great time and doesn't want to leave. Tough decision, but he opts for hell.

When he arrives to move in, however, he finds everything changed beyond recognition. There's a scorching desert, miserable people, and endless meaningless tasks to perform. "Hey," the guy says to the devil, "What's up with this? Yesterday, this place was great."

"Oh," responds the devil, "You were here on recruiting day. Now you're an employee." Don't let your office be a punchline. Help make each new employee's transition easier.

CARROT ACTION: Reconsider how you treat new people who join your team. What can you do to be more welcoming to ease what might be a difficult transition, and help them get up to speed faster?

White Board

Spray it, don't say it.

⌒〜

Graffiti, with erasable markers, not spray paint, on a white board is the fastest, easiest, and cheapest way to shoot out a shout-out to a co-worker worthy of praise.

Nearly every meeting room is surrounded by them, and you probably have one or two hanging around your department. Use them to spread the message of thanks and praise to your teammates. What's more, write up a quick message to or about someone in another department, or on the other side of the building. Let others know just how great so and so is from your area.

Start tagging the place today and watch the baby Carrots go viral as other people get the bug and start doing it as well. Get creative with where you can tag your thanks. It's low risk, high reward vandalism that usually doesn't involve the law.

CARROT ACTION: Take a non-permanent marker with you and go soil some virgin white boards. Remember to make your post specific.

Whoever You Are

Before God we are all equally wise—and equally foolish.
—Albert Einstein

There's a wonderful *New Yorker* cartoon by James Stevenson that depicts a vast office with desks pushed together in endless rows of lower-level employees. All are men wearing suits and shuffling papers on their desks. Into the scene breezes their balding boss, with a smile on his face, waving a cigar in one hand and patting an employee on the shoulder with the other. He says, "Keep up the good work, whatever it is, whoever you are."

No matter what your position is in the company, there are probably hierarchies of power above and below you. Just as the CEO can show condescending behavior, so can you. Don't do it. Treat everyone in your organization well. Be fair. Furthermore, show your appreciation by writing a quick note, complimenting people, and mentioning their good work to those who have responsibility for them. You don't have to be their boss to make a difference.

CARROT ACTION: Write a specific note today to thank someone for his or her great work. Consider especially those who are least likely to be noticed and make sure they know that they matter too. To start, make an effort to learn everyone's names on your floor—the mail people, the security personnel, the folks at the other end of the hall. Then use their names when praising their efforts.

Remember Special Days

Happy Birthday, Stella.

Never let a co-worker's birthday pass without giving him a card or other expression—taking the person to lunch, bringing him a cup of coffee in the morning, or some other special demonstration. Make sure the expression is specific to that person's tastes—for example, don't get coffee for someone who doesn't drink it.

Letting your people know you care about them as individuals is a sure-fire way to build a team environment and foster greater camaraderie.

CARROT ACTION: Enter the birthdays of your co-workers in a calendar and never let one of the dates pass without a card or other expression.

A Paradox

Life's a voyage that's homeward bound.
—Herman Melville

Work demands more from you than ever before but plays a smaller role in individual fulfillment. The consequence is a conflict between a desire to have your physical needs met (the paycheck) and to have your emotional needs meet (the payoff).

Brook Manville and Josiah Ober wrote in the *Harvard Business Review*, "We live today in a knowledge economy. The core assets of the modern business enterprise lie not in buildings, machinery, and real estate, but in the intelligence, understanding, skills, and experience of employees. Harnessing the capabilities and commitment of knowledge workers is . . . the central managerial challenge of our time."

As it grows more difficult to separate work and private life, we need to discover techniques of time-management and partition that support whole-life success.

CARROT ACTION: You have a financial budget, now create a whole-life budget. Note your time spent at home and at work, but be sure to include cross-over hours: time spent at home (but working) and at work (dealing with issues from home). If you find yourself over-absorbed with work, find a way to cut an hour or two out to devote fully to family or hobbies.

Making Decisions in the Dark

Making good choices when the way isn't clear.

You don't have to possess superhuman powers to make wise decisions in business. What you *do* need is an unwavering commitment to spend the time and energy necessary to figure it out. If there is any question if something is right or wrong, or if this decision will impact your integrity, you can't just say, "maybe it's okay." A trustworthy person finds out by asking trusted peers, supervisors, or consulting the right resources.

Those inklings (triggered by our instinct or conscience) can come at the most inconvenient times. If we listen, they require us to slow down and reconsider our decision with people we trust—even if minutes count. In a hurry to move forward, we quiet these important warning signals by telling ourselves, "No one will ever know," or "I'm just doing what management would want me to do," or "I'll do it differently next time." Usually phrases like these are used to make ourselves feel better about a decision that simply does not sit right. Don't let this happen to you.

CARROT ACTION: The next time you find yourself facing a decision that doesn't feel right, that's the precise moment to slow down and take a second look, and confer with others you trust.

Carrots Basics Reminder

Frequency.

Just as your spouse or significant other never tires of hearing you express your love and affection (as long as it's sincere, of course!), neither do your associates get sick of regular praise, gratitude, and recognition.

Frequency may just be the most difficult part of a concerted recognition strategy. You simply can't start building a Carrot Culture and then expect it to sustain itself. If you give a shout-out to a cube mate in a staff meeting or offer to give up your tickets to a ball game to someone who really achieved, plan to keep it up regularly.

Authentic, sincere recognition never gets old.

CARROT ACTION: Think of the last time you extended recognition to someone. Now go and do it again.

What Do You Want Them to Remember?

Make the right decisions before the decision arises.

One of the most memorable moments in television history occurred when Roberto Benigni won the Best Actor Oscar for his role in the movie *Life Is Beautiful*. Benigni jumped on his chair and threw his fists into the air. He ran down the aisle and bounced up the stairs, just about crushing Sophia Loren with his hug. The moment was full of the sheer joy of a man who had overcome unbelievable odds.

We can all do better at presenting awards to co-workers. Whether we are thanking someone with a free cup of morning coffee for helping us out yesterday, or presenting a service award for ten years of dedication, we should ask, "How can I make this presentation something this person will remember?"

A simple way is to tell a story using SAIL. Recount a Situation the person helped with, explain the Action they took and the Impact it had on the organization, then Link the story back to the goals of the company.

CARROT ACTION: The next time you have the chance to make comments during a co-worker's award presentation, make sure to prepare. Choose your words carefully and make sure that when it is all over and done that they will remember that they are valued and important.

Did you build the wall?

*How a blank slate might be what you need
to get to your goal.*

We all have plans and timelines. Yet most of us hit some type of wall that prevents us from reaching some of our goals. Our excuses are typically valid, but right now you're frustrated—especially because you knew the wall you've just hit would appear the day you began pursuing your goal.

Goal setting is a powerful tool—often requiring strategic maneuvers to overcome real hurdles and challenges. But sometimes those of us who are closest to our goals are actually the worst innovators of pursuit.

Walls need climbing sometimes. Other times they might just be distractions—glaring down at us and challenging us to climb over them when realistically our goal lies in a different direction. Maybe the wall is really just a guide. Ultimately it forces us to walk around it, where we'll realize that a bigger goal awaits—not over the wall, but at the end of the wall. Sometimes we achieve great things getting over these walls.

CARROT ACTION: Define your hurdles today. Instead of staring at them, ask a friend to take a look. That person might offer a simple solution that you never saw before.

He Said, She Said

*The best way to get yourself in trouble
is to misquote your boss, or Darth Vader.*
—Adrian Gostick and Chester Elton

⌒

The commands come from the top. Let's say leadership institutes a new policy in the following way. The CEO tells his senior executive team, "Let the people know that we no longer allow our folks to wear white socks with black shoes. It looks silly. We're also no longer selling double flange hinges in our stores."

The executive team disperses—relaying the message to their management teams, who then relay the message to the staff members. "Anyone caught wearing white socks while selling double flange hinges will be fired."

Anytime you're relaying information, find a way to ensure the correct information is passed along.

Even some of the most popular sayings of our generation are misquoted. Darth Vader never said, "Luke, I *am* your father." The actual quote was, "No, I am your father."

To effectively communicate a consistent message, put it in writing—email or a handwritten note is fine.

CARROT ACTION: Be honest when you relay information. Let people know that you may not have all the facts, but let them know where they can find all the information, and know where the information is stored so you can access it quickly.

Eddie Money Is a Problem

The distractions of love and cell phones.

George was a single, strapping advertising executive. He was focused, client-centric, and passionate about creating results. He worked long hours, and so he didn't have much of a social life. It's not surprising that he was viewed as "the go to guy" within the agency.

Then, George met Emily (surprise!). Hey, love happens—even to workaholics. And, it's a fantastic thing. However, Emily liked to occupy George's time on the cell phone, and through numerous text messages.

Is George to blame? Should he not have a social life?

George's major mistake was setting Emily's ringtone to play Eddie Money's "I Think I'm in Love" every time she called. It drove George's co-workers crazy. And it really bothered George's boss.

Ring tones communicate. George's told a distracting story that his boss had to nip in the bud. Use discretion.

CARROT ACTION: Understand the cell phone culture in your workplace, and until you're completely comfortable, set your phone on vibrate.

But No One Did It for Me

Two wrongs don't make a right.

We often hear businesspeople say the reason they don't recognize others is that they never received any recognition themselves—and they turned out just fine. If you were never recognized, that is regrettable, but it doesn't mean those around you should be cheated, too

If you feel this way, take the time to consider how much it would have meant to you as you rose through the ranks for someone to have given you the recognition you deserved. Then think about those who work for you, or colleagues on your team, whom you should be giving more recognition to.

CARROT ACTION: Make up for past slights you feel by making sure co-workers feel great about their accomplishments. Thank someone today by picking up some of their work, talking them up to the boss, or simply thanking them in person.

Take Notes

It works better than a string on your finger.

When you learn things about your co-workers—like their birthdays or favorite restaurant, or that they are vegetarians or don't drink or love Denzel Washington—take notes. You think you'll remember it all, but trust us, you won't. And that knowledge will pay dividends when you need to find a way to reward them later.

In one excellent recognition presentation we witnessed, co-workers knew the employee in the spotlight was a huge Billy Joel fan. A group of about ten took the music from one of his hits, changed the lyrics to brag about this person, and sang to her. The employee was in hysterics and the cheers were so deafening that the company's executive team came out of a meeting and asked that the song be repeated. It was, twice more.

CARROT ACTION: Start to carry a small, pocket-sized notepad just for this purpose. Or make it a point to return to your desk and enter the information into the computer. It doesn't matter how you do it, so long as you write it down.

The Psychological Importance of Esteem

The role in success of being needed.

American psychologist Abraham Maslow defined the five psychological needs of man: at the base level, survival (food, water, sleep, breath); next, safety (security, employment, health, property); then, relationships; fourth is a need for self-esteem; and finally, the urge to achieve the most we can, manifested in problem solving, creativity, lack of prejudice, and morality.

Work life is a major part of Maslow's hierarchy. Our jobs give us security. They enable us to acquire the necessities of survival. Our social networks on the job provide a portion of our need to belong.

To our point of view, a missing corporate link is on the level Maslow describes as esteem. Gaining respect and respecting others, growing in confidence by achievement: those are elements that recognition addresses. When an organization acknowledges the positive experiences of an employee and elevates that person in a social setting, the individual internalizes the achievement. Esteem builds and transforms into something larger and even more tangible.

CARROT ACTION: Address each level of Maslow's hierarchy separately by asking questions of yourself and how each of the human needs is being met. Then, think about improvements you could make in your own life or in improving the lives of your co-workers.

Tell Her About It

Don't trickle down compliments.

Your friend Amy is handling a tough project at work remarkably well. You've noticed and you're impressed. So you tell friend Breanne who mentions it to friend Conner, who posts it on his blog. Friend Darren reads that and tells his wife, who happens to run into Amy at the gym and says, "I heard somewhere that you're handling that project at work remarkably well."

To which Amy says, "Who did you hear that from?" And Darren's wife replies, "I don't remember. But good job!"

CARROT ACTION: Make every compliment mean something by telling the person yourself. She'll love that you noticed, and she'll appreciate your personal approach and vote of confidence. Your kind words might just be the push she needs to get through the worst of challenges.

Feed 'Em and Weep

The easiest way to people's hearts is through their pie hole.

⌒

If you make "killer" chocolate chip cookies, share the love and bring a couple dozen to work. Is your chili really a blue ribbon winning concoction? Heat it up in the break room and clang the dinner bell (email blast). If you create French crepes so thin and delicious that your children will actually clean their rooms just to gaze upon them, by all means part out the pancakes with your peers.

Food rewards say more than just "thanks" or "well done," they also say "I am aware of how terrific you are, and what's more, I'm still thinking about it when I'm pulling homemade bread out of the oven at home: enjoy!"

One woman working for a catering company reported to us that when her team hits goals she brings in her "world famous" spaghetti from home to celebrate. Her teammates go nuts for it and as they share the spoils it draws them closer together.

Even people working *with* food still love to *get* food.

CARROT ACTION: Surprise your team tomorrow with your heavenly brownies.

Reputation

Once lost it is difficult to regain.

Here's a positive reality of working: no matter how engaged or disengaged we are at work, we all affect the company. Admittedly some of us help more than others.

Now, here's a sad truth of working. While we all contribute to our organization's success, every one of us has much more potential to hurt our organizations than we have to help it. One mistake in judgment, one dishonorable action, could hurt the firm's reputation in irreparable ways.

In a company, the assets are not only capital and equipment, but the employees and its reputation. Any of those can be diminished by outside or inside forces, but the last is the hardest to regain. So take exquisite care in all of the decisions you make.

CARROT ACTION: Perform every action with the thought that it could be written up tomorrow on the front page of the newspaper.

Porch Swing Personnel

*Happiness is when what you think, what you say,
and what you do are in harmony.*
—Mahatma Gandhi

We know a man who made a ton of money for his firm with his new ideas and energy. He was rewarded financially for his success with a large salary, and he spent the rest of his career relaxing—coming in to work, but doing little or nothing.

Was he satisfied? He was happy to cash the paycheck. Was he engaged? No.

In your organization, right now, there are plenty of employees who are satisfied. The problem with mere satisfaction is that it doesn't engender passion.

Over time, unfulfilled promise starts to eat at us. The human spirit feels best when we accomplish, stretch, risk.

The ideal is a workforce that is both satisfied and engaged.

CARROT ACTION: Give yourself a satisfaction vs. engaged quiz. Where would you place yourself, right now: unengaged and unsatisfied; highly engaged but unsatisfied; unengaged yet highly satisfied; or highly engaged and highly satisfied? If you need an engagement boost, set clear goals that align with the company and hold yourself accountable for hitting them.

Shooting Higher

Be not simply good; be good for something.
—Henry David Thoreau

There's a bumper sticker that reads, "Well-behaved women seldom make history." And, in many prominent cases, it seems to be true.

Princess Diana was once publicly scolded for being too "public."

Mother Theresa was questioned for not asking for permission.

Oprah has been condemned for "having too much influence."

And yet each woman changed the world for the better because she shot higher than expectations.

When setting a goal, aim higher than the rules, because "meets expectations" rarely gets rewarded.

CARROT ACTION: Make noise today. We're not condoning mischief, but suggesting actions that exceed expectations. If the boss asks for two of something, offer four. If your team says, "That'll do," say "We can do better."

Simon Says

When Your Job Is Listening.

If you ask most people how good they are at communication, you'll receive varied responses, but most of them will believe that they're above average. Now, ask people how good they are at listening. You'll hear a different set of responses, with many people admitting that they are poor listeners.

The game Simon Says exposes a concept that is difficult for many people to master—the difference between hearing and listening. Everybody playing the game hears what Simon says. Yet all of the players don't listen, take in to account, and respond the same way. (If they did, they might actually *win* American Idol. Oh, wait, wrong Simon.)

Half of communication is listening. And we all could use some work on it from time to time.

So listen carefully. *Simon says* listen carefully.

CARROT ACTION: Make it a point today to communicate nearly exclusively with questions. Force others to do all the talking simply so you can work on your skills as a listener. Recognize their communication by listening and responding only with follow-up questions.

The Grudge

It's not a good look on you.

⌒

Are you holding a grudge? Be honest. Do you have a friend, family member, or co-worker who—about a million years ago—did or said something that angered you, and you still dislike them because of it? He's a decent, smart, successful person, but his opinions differed and continue to differ from yours, so you refuse to acknowledge that his perspectives are valid. You are going to make him suffer by ignoring him, disparaging him to his boss, and maybe mocking him behind his back. Aren't you exhausted?

So he had a different opinion; he didn't like your idea; he expressed concern over your pet project. But is it worth it to hold this grudge?

The next time your friend or co-worker or family member offers a perspective that you don't like, don't take it personally. It's your chance to look at a situation from a different angle—and that can only make us better and stronger as individuals.

Lose any grudges you might hold.

CARROT ACTION: Today, make it a priority to track down your "grudges." Walk to their cubicle, make a phone call, or visit them tonight. A simple, sincere "How have you been?" will work wonders.

Your Opinion, Please

Recognition can be a matter of opinion.

In the United States taxes are due today. No one at the Internal Revenue Service has ever asked if their customers think this is okay. You, on the other hand, can ask for feedback at work by asking for opinions on projects you are working on. This shows co-workers that their ideas are important and valid and, of course, you'll get some great ideas you wouldn't have thought of on your own.

Broaching the topic will get easy in time. The first step is to ask someone for an opinion. The second is to try to incorporate at least one suggestion, but then show her the result. That way, the co-worker will be very willing next time to contribute again.

CARROT ACTION: Today, ask two co-workers for their opinions on your most important project. Listen attentively and try to incorporate some of their ideas, and be sure to give them credit.

Whiteboard Carrots

Getting to know you.

Camaraderie with teammates is built on knowledge. On a whiteboard somewhere in your department, put up pictures of your teammates and put a "get to know me" question at the top of the board.

We've seen things like, "What's your favorite movie?" and "What superhero power would you like to have?" and "What scares you more than anything else?"

Each co-worker writes his or her answer under her picture and the board is left for a week or more, giving other employees a chance to read it. Change the question regularly. Remember to keep it fun and clean.

CARROT ACTION: Just do it already. You don't need permission. Be the first one to do it.

Execution

Get the Job Done in Tenses.

It's just an idea until it's a plan. It's just a plan until it's executed.

Different people with different job titles focus on different portions of any process. Ken Blanchard, co-author of *The One Minute Manager*, once said, "I decided a while ago that the present and the future are crashing into each other. Companies need to manage the present, and create the future. And, sadly, most companies make the mistake of having the same people handle both tasks."

Think of accountability in tenses: Plan, Planning, Planned. Execute, Executing, and Executed.

Use this system to divide stages of progress among employees. And don't be shocked if you, like Blanchard, realize that different people are stronger at one stage of the process than another.

CARROT ACTION: To get a better feel for each of the stages, play in only the future tense today and just plan. Tomorrow, play in the active present—execute only. Finally, take an entire day to operate in the past tense—in which you measure your execution. Get a good feel for all of the tenses you will at some point work in. Understanding each of the phases will help you organize your days.

The Next Six Weeks

What does your near future hold?

We can't change the weather, but we can control the next six weeks as we move towards our goal. In fact, six weeks is a perfect amount of time to accomplish something magnificent—the development of a ritual.

Habits can be formed by daily repetition over the course of about two and a half weeks. Good habits can also be broken quite quickly—some experts say all it takes is about three to four days of discontinuation.

But can a ritual be just as easily broken? A ritual is something that becomes ingrained in us, and has a purpose that's often bigger than the act itself. For example, one ritual is to bow your head before eating and give thanks for the food. In fact, the word ritual is often tied to spiritual practices—things that we believe touch our soul. And, your goals should be included in that category.

Take the next six weeks to establish your new ritual, a new work or life goal that will become part of your life going forward.

CARROT ACTION: Invest in three calendars—one for exercise routines, one for goal setting, and one for other business and personal appointments. Make a ritual of sitting down each night with your stack of calendars to write in what you'll do and what you've done. Why three separate calendars? Each one deserves equal focus and separate attention.

You're Being Watched

*Treat your co-workers, bosses, employees,
and customers like trusted partners.*

Do you feel like your every move is watched? Like someone is carefully observing your actions, scrutinizing your words, *and* analyzing your motives?

If so, you're not crazy. You're employed. People really *are* watching you. A trustworthy employee knows this and only makes decisions that he wouldn't mind being scrutinized by anyone.

While we all operate in business with a set of rules, the trouble is that the goalposts move now and then as society changes. That's why we must ask ourselves not only what are the rules, but whether they can be exposed to the light of day. How would this practice look if it were covered this afternoon on CNN? Even if everybody in your industry does it, think about how this might look to the people who might be watching you.

CARROT ACTION: Get in the habit of telling your boss, co-workers, and family members the good news and the bad. Take the blame when it's your fault. Act like you're being watched at all times.

Find a Cause

And give.

Raja Ali drives for Summit Limo in New Jersey. When we need a driver, we always ask for Raja.

As we were driving to the airport one day, Raja gifted us the book, *Three Cups of Tea*. The hero of this true story is Greg Mortenson, who raises money to build schools in the most remote parts of Pakistan and Afghanistan for children who would not otherwise receive an education. Greg believes that educated people are much less likely to join radical movements.

We adopted Mortenson's charity, the Central Asia Institute, and so far our Carrot friends have just about helped us raise enough money to build an entire school.

When you support a charity and get everyone in your organization involved, it promotes pride. Everyone wants to work harder for an organization that cares about its community and the world at large.

CARROT ACTION: Find a charity that is worthy of your support and get your team involved. Start looking today.

Quiet Leaders

Telling people you're honest is like boasting of your humility.

⌒

If you've ever told someone how honest you are, then you probably lied. Honesty isn't something you can claim, like a fancy title. It's a judgment made by the people around you based on your actions.

People who talk about their personal integrity typically put us on alert. A used car salesman who lets you know he's never sold a defective vehicle should raise the hairs on the back of anyone's neck.

Honest people right or prevent moral wrongs in the workplace inconspicuously and usually without casualties. Ethicists call these people quiet leaders because their modesty and restraint are in large measure responsible for their extraordinary achievements.

Humble, quiet leaders are also considerate and courteous. They do the little things that win friends and admirers. They smile and greet co-workers every day, they reflect on how their decisions will affect others, they praise and recognize their employees and even their bosses, they control their tempers, and they allow others to be kind to them.

In other words, they act like their moms taught them to all those years ago.

CARROT ACTION: The next time you have the urge to tell a customer, boss, or family member how honest you are, keep it to yourself. Actions speak louder than words.

Who Do You Trust?

Early men learned to distrust. Businessmen do the same.

How do you recognize a trustworthy person? It's harder than you might think. Maybe it's cynicism. Maybe it's negativism. Whatever the reason, we're typically better at detecting potential scoundrels or people we don't trust than we are at identifying trustworthy individuals.

Psychologists say this might stem from man's development. The types of humans that survived early in our evolution had early warning systems for reliability and trust that we still possess.

Today, one of the big markers we humans use is this: does a person follow through and do what she has promised? If so, we quickly put our stamp of approval on her. If not, we don't trust that person.

Now just because you hit deadlines doesn't mean you'll be completely trusted, you must still think for yourself, handle complicated situations, and make wise decisions when issues arise. But making good on a commitment is a window on our integrity, and that provides people with an ideal indicator of trustworthiness.

Carrot Action: Always do what you say you will do. Realize that others are judging your trustworthiness based on your ability to live up to your promises.

The Greater Good

*What happens when you care about others
more than yourself?*

⌐⌐

What goes around comes around. Even today in the hectic twenty-first century, this ancient truth has validity. It is not at all naïve to think that you should look out for the team and organization to which you belong, care about the products and services you produce, and watch out for your teammates. And in turn, you will gain a greater sense of purpose and peace in your life.

Okay, maybe you've had a boss from hell, a co-worker who stole all your ideas, or a neighbor who was laid off a year before retirement. "I have to look out for myself," you might be saying.

While there are a fair share of demagogues and abusers out there, on the whole if you are committed to your organization, and if you make decisions that benefit your teammates (even above your own gain), you will succeed in the long term. If you don't believe that, then there is a very good chance you have been working in a diseased environment. A major goal of this book is to help you foster a healthy environment in which everyone succeeds through teamwork.

CARROT ACTION: Before you make your next business decision, take this experiment. Count how many people around you the decision will impact. Chances are you'll see that your actions affect more people than you might have initially thought.

Finding the Good

If your honesty needs a boost, find a mentor.

While we'd like to believe that all of us are inherently good, our upbringing either enhances and brings out that goodness, or, sadly, suppresses it. The easiest time in life to learn how to be a person of integrity is when you're very young in your home, from your parents or other role models. That's not always possible.

So what if, upon honest reflection, you find that your innate "goodness" turns out to be more on the suppressed side? The key is finding a mentor.

It's certainly possible to learn these values through a mentor. Sometimes it's a teacher, sometimes a coach, sometimes a boss or co-worker. And the sooner you start, the better.

All of us are innately good, are naturally attracted to good, but we all need role models and teaching. The earlier that that can happen in your life and career, the better off you will be.

CARROT ACTION: If you are early in your career, ask someone you respect to be your mentor for a year. If you have a few years under your belt, ask a younger employee if he or she needs any advice to help them figure out the inner workings of the company.

Selflessness

What drives you is evident in your behavior.

One CEO we spoke with talked about a team member he once hired. The new employee took part of every day to call the finance department to see what his stock options were worth. It was clear to everyone what this man valued most.

The most noticeable characteristic of a trusted person is a degree of selflessness. In hiring or promoting someone, many leaders will consider what drives him or her. Is it personal gain or is it the welfare of teammates, customers, and the organization at large? The answer is usually evident in a person's behavior.

Most successful people have committed to bettering the company or team versus furthering a personal agenda. The selfless mind-set will not only keep you out of trouble, but give you the respect of your leaders and co-workers.

An attitude of devotion doesn't mean others will take advantage of you. A person with integrity lives with humility and an eye toward others, but can still be successful and well rewarded. In fact, a person with integrity is typically a much better potential leader, and distinguishes himself as such.

CARROT ACTION: Ask yourself: Do I spend my time thinking about my teammates/spouse/friends and their needs, or just my own?

It's Time to Stop

To make good decisions, take time to reflect.

Just stop. Stop racing around. Stop answering the phone. Stop worrying about the most recent crisis at work. Find an hour of uninterrupted time for some serious self-evaluation. It helps if things are quiet in your office. It helps if you can be alone. It helps if you don't feel rushed.

Finding an oasis of personal time may possibly be one of the greatest challenges of our hectic lives, but it's one of the most important. You have to put some effort into reflection when faced with difficult choices.

Some successful people use the same hour each day, others have to schedule just a few minutes of contemplation time once or twice a week, some we spoke with use their commute time on the train or by turning off the radio in the car. The point is, it's important to force yourself to listen.

CARROT ACTION: Every week take at least an hour or two and find a quiet place to reflect on what your intuitions may be telling you. Behind your desk with your eyes closed may not be ideal, but a long walk at lunch might be.

Capture the Moment

Take a picture, it'll last longer.

⌒⌒

We've seen so many powerful award ceremonies, and we've been a part of some fun ones too. But the human brain can remember only so many moments. That's why we encourage others to take pictures of a recognition award ceremony and give them to the recipient. This is a great way to involve the person's family, as his loved ones finally get to see what the boss and other co-workers look like.

Photos create a great memory for the employee as well as serving as a constant motivator to achieve more.

CARROT ACTION: During the next award presentation, take pictures and put them in a frame. They will be treasured for years to come.

You Never "Mentor" Be So Awesome

Tap the mentor in you.

Some people respond to responsibility like icing on a cupcake.

Pick someone (if you're in a position of responsibility) to mentor a new hire. Or, if you're not a "boss," how about picking someone to mentor you?

Expressing this confidence in the person and his skill set, knowledge, experience or personality can be a *huge* boost to his confidence and/or his motivation. Just by saying, "teach me," you put him in a great position to exceed your expectations.

Don't do it just to add to his work load, though. Make sure that he knows you believe he'll do a great job. And make sure he gets back to you if it gets to be too much. This means you need to be sure to check in frequently for status updates.

CARROT ACTION: Make sure your pick will be the kind of person who can, and will, follow through. This is an important relationship.

To Be Brutally Honest

Tough conversations build trust and respect.

One thing remains constant from Europe to Asia: a person who has high standards has the utmost respect for his or her teammates. No matter where you are in the world, trusted people treat others exactly how they would like to be treated: honestly and fairly.

That kind of respect can mean being honest but kind with your teammates and employees when necessary. Again, we're not talking about cruelty—"Wow that dress really shows you've gained a few pounds"—but being honest about performance issues.

Many well-intended businesspeople never have tough conversations with their co-workers, bosses, or employees. In an attempt to avoid hurting anyone's feelings, these people say only supportive, nice things.

Teams made up of individuals like this fail to have honest debates, and eventually reach a point where they fail to grow.

CARROT ACTION: Make a list of the things that bother you at work. Now pare it back to five, then three, then one. Gather those involved and have a tough conversation about the problem. Go to the meeting with suggestions on how to fix the challenge, and the result will be a win-win.

Least. Favorite. Job.

If they hate to do it, maybe you can hate it a little less.

You know how you have that thing at work you just hate to do? You know exactly when it's coming and conveniently get sick that day.

Find out what that thing is for someone else, and volunteer to do it.

Sounds crazy, but hopefully it won't be as bad for you as it is for her, and the loyalty and trust you create from doing it will offset the bitter taste.

Want a great team-building exercise? Let others know you're doing it. Invite them to watch as you clean out the recycling bin, replace the water jug, or call that nasty customer. As they stand and make fun of you for whatever it is you're going through, you can smile on the inside knowing the grief you've spared your friend.

CARROT ACTION: The nastier the job, the larger the effect. Really dig in and inspire your team. Mike Rowe's got nothing on you!

Write It Down

Shock everyone with your knowledge.

We all know that recognition means the most when it's personal. We also know that when we recognize our co-workers the team becomes more cohesive and successful. But how are you supposed to get to know each co-worker on a more "personal" level? First of all, you have a lot of co-workers, and second of all, some of them you really *don't* want to get to know you on a personal level.

So make it easy. When you hear or notice random facts about a person—he loved the brownies you brought in or she *really* loves Julia Roberts's movies—write them down. Just keep a little notebook or file with little tidbits of info for later use. Then when it is time for recognition, your knowledge will be invaluable. And the teammate that you're recognizing will appreciate the fact that you've been paying attention.

CARROT ACTION: Create that file or buy that notebook today. You'll be surprised at how much you can learn about your co-workers just by paying attention. Your first recognition presentation is going to be a hit.

Talking Heads

Your product is a chatterbox.

⌐⌐

Some people are great orators. Some are great teachers. Some are great entertainers. And some are just smooth talkers.

Good communication counts for a lot, but results speak volumes. A great "sales representative" isn't great unless her numbers are great. A great manager is not great because he sounds like a manager, dresses like a manager, and has a grand title, he's great because the people he manages call him a great manager.

Think about the product of "you"—it's doing a whole lot of talking whether or not you're in the room with it. The question is what's it saying?

CARROT ACTION: Put your product to the test. Ask a new audience (perhaps a few people you've just met or, better yet, a career coach) to review the things that you do, build, create, manage, or implement.

Ask or Tell

Stumped? Start talking.

⌒

When Adrian once made a mistake with math, his thirteen-year-old son Tony quipped (with dripping sarcasm), "Don't worry, Dad. Numbers are hard." Well, here are some really hard numbers to take: Only one-third of workers believe that their employer knows what motivates them to perform well and produce high-quality work.

In addition, slightly less than half of managers admit they don't know how to motivate the employees they supervise.

So what to do? *Start talking.* If you are a manager, call in your employees one by one and ask what types of recognition they would most enjoy. If you are an employee, let your boss know the type of recognition that works for you. Managers will get the answers they need, and employees will feel better appreciated.

CARROT ACTION: In your next performance review, take the opportunity to express to your manager how you like to be recognized.

Honest Examples

Teaching the next generation to make good choices starts with your actions.

Any businessperson will tell you that it's hard to teach honesty to someone who's already in the workplace. Honest behavior should be taught first and foremost in the home. But any parent will admit it's hard to raise kids who make the right decisions when faced with tough choices, kids who will not buckle under pressure.

The key to raising honest children is personal example. Parents can talk about it, but real teaching is done through example over time. Children notice behavior more than words. They'll notice if a clerk gives you the wrong change and you walk away and say, "That clerk gave me five dollars too much! Aren't I lucky?" Endeavor to be a paragon of honesty in all of your dealings, and you will see your good example reflected in your children.

CARROT ACTION: If you want to teach your kids to be honest, make a commitment yourself to never lie, exaggerate, or tell only part of the facts (for instance, why you or your child is missing a day of work or school). It's hard, but well worth the effort.

Family Focus

The only thing we love more than ourselves is our kids.

Ever get lemon-faced when someone brags about his kids at work? Why not make lemonade and do his bragging for him?

Designate a poster board or display area for Family Focus. Post pictures, report cards, college acceptance letters, random exploits, and so on, and let your employees' kids (or their families) shine. For those without kids, pictures of their dogs work well. Cats too. You could also let someone's hobbies or community service take the spotlight. Believe it or not, some people don't like to brag. You need to do it for them.

CARROT ACTION: Designate someone (or yourself) as the keeper of the board. Weekly or monthly updates become a welcome, anticipated topic of conversation. It would also be a good idea to be the first person to post a few things to encourage participation.

Go

Make your life a mission, not an intermission.

When Andrew Lipinsky arrived for his job interview, he understood the impact that day could have on the rest of his life. The pressure was on, and so were the cameras—watching his every movement to help the producers of the hit television show *The Apprentice* determine if Lipinksy would be a contestant that season.

Lipinsky was a debate champion in college. He was charming, smart, and the youngest applicant to be considered. Yet he was at a huge disadvantage to the other applicants—his actual job experience paled in comparison.

The producers shared their concerns with Lipinsky, and he knew that this was his one chance to change his life forever. At that moment he told himself, "Go." He started talking, persuading, and let his personality shine. The effect? The producers gave him a shot. What are the defining moments of your future?

Andrew became a contestant. Will you say go in your life?

CARROT ACTION: Goal setting is often about actions to be done in the future. But we recommend that today you command yourself. Say the word "go" before every action. Work like you're driving a race car. Win your race. And, when you move to your next task, drop a new flag.

In the Company of Elephants

Talk about the heavy issues first.

Imagine an elephant is wandering through your cubical maze at work, squishing Madge's purse, stepping on Frank's key fob. The animal is causing problems, but nobody wants to acknowledge it.

Many of us take the same attitude of disregard to serious or negative topics in the workplace. Take Stacy, a manager at an insurance company who was well aware that one of her employees wasn't performing as expected. Files were misplaced. Deadlines were missed. The employee had already received "soft" warnings during performance reviews.

It was decided on a Monday that the employee must be terminated. Most of the team knew it was coming. But not wanting to hurt the employee's feelings, Stacy decided she would break the news on Friday afternoon—after the team luncheon, so the employee could enjoy one more group event. Can you imagine the elephant in the room all week?

Avoiding direct discussion about heavy issues doesn't mean the issues don't exist. The elephant in the office diminishes everyone's capacity to achieve their own goals.

CARROT ACTION: Get the heavy issues out on the table. Sure, feelings will get hurt sometimes. But the more direct we are about weighty topics, the sooner the issues can be resolved.

A Dedication to Their . . . Dedication

On-air carrots.

Is your office one of those places that's always got a radio on? Why not let your favorite morning DJ express some appreciation? Call in to your office's favorite morning show and tell them what's up. Single out an individual or group for something they've done or being consistently great.

CARROT ACTION: Spend a second finding a song that really fits your group's personality, or work ethic, or something funny that happened at work, and send it around to everyone with a brief note explaining its relevance.

Hiring Character

*The best way to predict how someone will act
is to look at what they've done.*

It's easy to learn a new computer program or new company policies. Even language barriers can be overcome given time. But it is very difficult to train a new employee to be trustworthy.

While it is possible to enhance your trust level at any age, that journey is very personal and cannot be prescribed by an employer. That's one reason many leaders promote people from inside their organizations.

After all, the best way to predict what someone's going to do in the future is to know what they've done in the past—the way they addressed difficult issues or dealt with people around them. You may be able to put on a certain face for a week, but you can't hide who you are for five years.

A leader once told us, "When you go outside to hire you always get a surprise. Sometimes it's a good surprise. But you never hire quite the person you thought you were hiring."

CARROT ACTION: Ask yourself: When I'm involved in hiring a new teammate or employee, what should I look for? Experience and skills, or character? What questions can I ask to determine someone's moral fiber?

Recycled Recognition

Your reputation precedes you. Again.

We've all got thank-you letters or congratulations cards or simple awards sitting in a drawer of our desk. Take them out and post or place them in a place for all to see. Like a war hero displaying his medals proudly upon his chest, such a shrine can really bring out the moxie in people.

Past achievements, letters from great customer service moments, posting these is a great way to let the rest of the office in on what you already know.

CARROT ACTION: Encourage people around you to show off their recognition *stuff* and relive the glory days. It may inspire them to do it again.

Coachability

Not a real word, but a great way to learn.

Two of the best compliments you can be given in the workplace are: (1) that you do "great work" (there's no substitute for someone who can just flat out deliver), and (2) that you are "coachable."

When you are coachable you are open to new ideas, to improvement, to the possibility of a better way of doing things. You are able to check your ego at the door, and because of that the payoff is large.

Here's another benefit of being coachable: When it's your turn to give constructive coaching to others, they are much more open to your suggestions.

One simple way to become more coachable? Next time you are lost when driving, stop and ask for directions.

CARROT ACTION: If someone makes a suggestion about how to do something better today, listen, take notes, and thank them. They will feel more valued that you took them seriously, and you may end up with a great idea.

Ode to Team

Are you accountable to the team or for the team?

Teamwork is a concept that is still sometimes a mystery. It's been studied, analyzed, and practiced. It's been honed, emulated, and even perfected by various groups.

Many hockey fans consider the 1980 U.S. Olympic Hockey Team—otherwise referred to as the Miracle on Ice—as a perfect team. Others may recall political teams, business teams, or even teams in the movies.

The question is, when you're on a team, are you accountable to it or for it?

Teamwork, often a strategy that is more organic than forced, is a combination of personalities and passions bouncing off one another in synchronized fashion.

Bigger than explanation, great teams understand when they've achieved synchronicity—leaving the question between "to the team" and "for the team" unanswerable. Without doubt, in a well functioning team both answers are correct.

CARROT ACTION: Recognize the team you are on today, even if it's an unofficial team. Thank your spouse for all he or she does for "the team." Thank the security guard at the front door, the teller at the bank, and the server at your favorite restaurant. Thank the people in your life who make your life possible.

Dreaming Big

It's not just for children and Greek sculptors.

Pygmalion is a sculptor in Greek mythology who falls in love with a statue he carved out of ivory. According to the myth, his statue is so realistic that he begins to offer the statue gifts. Eventually Pygmalion prays to Aphrodite and begs her to make the statue come to life. Aphrodite shows pity, realizing his love for the statue is real, and grants his wish.

If we truly believe in something, can we make it happen? The Pygmalion theory and research data suggest that if goals are set higher than an expected level of achievement, people will perform to a greater level, even though they may not accomplish the goal.

CARROT ACTION: Pick the goal you struggle with the most to achieve. Now, make it harder—add another element, a tighter deadline, or a new level of quality. Announce to your peers that you're "Going Big." And then, run at that goal headfirst, having full knowledge that you may fail. But you'll make it further than you ever have in the past.

Uncommon Sense

*Common sense is the knack of seeing things as they are,
and doing things as they ought to be done.*
—C. E. Stowe

Common sense and goal setting shouldn't necessarily go hand in hand. To accelerate performance, uncommon sense is a necessity—not only seeing things as they are and doing things as they ought to be done, but also seeing and doing things as they could be done better.

Howard Hughes, the aviator, engineer, industrialist, film producer and director, philanthropist, and one of the wealthiest people in the world, also left a legacy for being eccentric and difficult to work with.

In Hughes's defense, goal setting and achieving are personal endeavors. They only belong to the individual who owns them.

CARROT ACTION: Play the "If I had it my way" game today. Play it on a personal level but also play it with your team. Ask your team to announce one of their goals and describe how they would see achievement if there were no boundaries.

Sales vs. Reputation

*What we can learn about reputation
from a* Newsweek *scoop?*

In the late 1990s, *Newsweek* was the first news organization to learn, from Linda Tripp, of the relationship between White House intern Monica Lewinsky and Bill Clinton, then president of the United States. It was not only a sensational scoop, but a story they knew would garner international attention and sell record numbers of magazine copies.

But the information had only one source: Linda Tripp. The reporter had been unable to talk to Lewinsky or the White House, and the magazine was going to press.

Like all ethical journalists, the editors were committed to a policy of not printing allegations of misconduct without giving the person accused a fair opportunity to reply. Thus, *Newsweek* decided not to print the story in the next issue, even though it was certain to appear in some publication during the following week. It was a highly principled decision, which certainly cost *Newsweek* in sales. But it was a decision made with integrity that benefited the magazine's reputation.

CARROT ACTION: It's hard to make the right decisions under pressure if you haven't defined your personal values well before challenges arise. Today, write your own ethical mission statement.

Listen and Prosper

Do your co-workers believe their opinions count?

When people feel valued, companies prosper. The Gallup Organization's multiyear research identified twelve key characteristics of successful workplaces—businesses in which employee retention, customer satisfaction, productivity, and profitability are at high levels.

"At work, my opinions seem to count," was one of those twelve, establishing a statistical link between employees feeling valued and company profitability.

CARROT ACTION: Remember that when your co-workers know that what they say matters and is making a difference, they are more engaged and more productive, which brings forth better ideas, energy, and camaraderie.

What Makes a Co-worker Tick?

Different strokes for different folks.

Are you caught up in "you"? Most of us are. In fact, have you ever felt sorry for yourself at work and said (insert whiney voice here), "Nobody around here cares about me or understands me!"

Is it possible that the reason none of your co-workers cares about you or understands you is because you haven't shown an interest in them? Do you care about or understand your co-workers? The guy in the cubicle next to you—what did he do over the weekend? The woman two cubes down—what has she been working on that has her coming in so early every morning? Why don't you find out?

By taking an interest in your co-workers, you'll be building team morale. Before long, your team will be bonding and you will be an integral part.

And, voilà, someone may start caring about you.

CARROT ACTION: Find out what makes your co-workers tick. Maybe the co-worker two cubes down would love a morning cup of coffee, maybe another would appreciate help on the phones for an hour. Show you care, and they will too.

Family Day

Get their loved ones involved.

Encourage your business to open to families at least one day a year, and make sure the boss is present and available all day to shake hands and thank co-workers and their loved ones in person.

The more family members understand and relate to the workplace, the more supportive they can be. Encourage employees groups to show off their latest work.

CARROT ACTION: Ask teams to show off their latest projects during the open house. And if all else fails, let the kids pop Bubble Wrap in shipping.

Send It Up

Don't forget to praise your boss.

⌒⌒

When we do radio call-in shows, one of the most frequently asked questions is, "My boss is terrible at recognition. How do I get him to start recognizing me?" One great way to start the cycle is by recognizing your boss for the good things he does.

Senior leaders need love, too. And a sincere note of thanks or verbal praise will go a long way. First, your boss will feel better about his role in the organization—knowing he is seen in a positive light by his employees. Second, he will begin to see the role recognition can play in motivating others, and will start to send some of the praise your way soon.

CARROT ACTION: Drop a note of thanks on your boss's desk today. Be specific in your thanks, explaining how he has helped you in the past month, and on which projects.

Mentor

*Seek out talented people above and below you
on the career ladder.*

It's tough to be the "new guy" at work. We've all been there. Take a new employee under your wing; be his mentor. You have the knowledge, the experience, and the know-how that he doesn't have—so share the wealth.

Make the job easier for your new co-worker by offering to answer any questions he may have regarding his new job duties and how to do them. Help him understand the company culture and lay of the land. Introduce him to everyone you can. You don't have to be attached at the hip, but make yourself available.

CARROT ACTION: Let the new guy know that you're available if he has questions or needs any help, and mean it. The relationships you forge as a mentor will benefit you for years, not only with that employee but with other co-workers and management.

New Mantra:
Change Is Good

Resistance is futile.

Do you make life easier or harder for your co-workers? When a new strategy, system, or way of doing things comes along, are you the person who accepts the new way and runs with it, or are you the team member who resists change, complains about it, drags her feet in learning it, and holds up the entire team? If you don't/won't learn the new way of doing things, you're slowing down the process and/or creating extra work for your teammates. Either way, nobody is pleased with you.

From now on, be the person who is flexible and open to change. Be the employee who learns the new way and teaches the rest of the team how to do it. You'll make yourself look better in the eyes of your co-workers and your boss. They'll see you as a resource instead of the source of frustration.

CARROT ACTION: Here's the Carrot for your boss and co-workers today: be willing to try someone's new idea or learn the new system without one complaint all day. Your willingness to "give in" will be noticed and appreciated.

In Praise of Tenacity

Let me tell you the secret that has led me to my goal:
my strength lies solely in my tenacity.
—Louis Pasteur

Every day socks perform the same function—clinging to your feet regardless of the hurdles they encounter. And, after each performance, they prepare for a brand new day—with the same vigor they had for the day before.

Socks just might be one of the most ideologically perfect inventions of all time—having the tenacity to perform superbly and the elasticity to adapt unconditionally.

They bear our weight, bend with our movement, and even allow us to change and grow. They take a beating in the spin cycle, rarely receive recognition, and still perform just like we expect.

Socks are consistent in their goals, yet able to adapt to almost any change.

CARROT ACTION: Tenacity and adaptability are considered by "management" as some of the most valuable traits. The next time you are faced with an obstacle, don't give up. Ask for help, search for solutions, and pull up your socks.

Positive Predictability

Steady as she goes.

Consistent people are predictable—in a good way. If you've known a consistent person, you can predict how she will react in most difficult situations. They are honest, constant, and eminently believable.

The hard part is, like love, you can't hurry consistency. It's proven over time. You, or your co-worker, may be able to show a certain face for a day, or even a week. But over a year or two or five you're going to show your colors.

Consistent people typically get to the point quickly, which saves a lot of time. They are confident and say what they believe, even if it's unpopular. Yet they rarely seem to hurt feelings. Why? Because their directness seems genuinely driven by a desire to see others succeed.

Consistency is the mark of a person who cannot be swayed by external forces: money; power; influence. His actions are inseparably connected to his inner moral values.

Some might argue that you can't truly be great if you are not consistent. And they'd be absolutely right.

CARROT ACTION: Ask yourself, "Can others predict how I'll react to certain situations based on my personal code of conduct?" If not, it's time to define your priorities and values.

Intent

"There's a sucker born every minute."
—P. T. Barnum

Without intent, there is no communication. All words and actions shared between two or more people have intent—a desired response or outcome from that communication.

P. T. Barnum, one of the world's greatest marketers, is said to be one of the first millionaire entertainers in history. Barnum promoted hoaxes, gimmicks, and tricks. He captured the amazement of the human imagination. And while he was probably the world's most famous "snake oil" pitchman, P. T. Barnum's customers rarely left dissatisfied.

Why? Because his customers almost always understood his intent—to entertain.

Communication in all other aspects of life shares the same rules. Managers may attempt to increase productivity. Loved ones may attempt to change behaviors, receive advice, or call for attention. Children may need assistance, comforting, and guidance. All are seeking a response to their communication—and satisfaction for "marketing" their intentions.

CARROT ACTION: Analyze the intentions of one conversation you have today. Maybe it's the maintenance worker who tells a joke. Maybe it's Phyllis in accounting who tells you that your expense reports are overdue. No matter who it is, take a deep look at the intent of their communication—because understanding intentions always leaves at least one "customer" completely satisfied.

Personalize Work

Recognize the new mom or dad.

It's important to let your co-workers know you care about them on a personal level, and to create a connection beyond the workplace. When an employee has a baby, it is a wonderful opportunity to send a thoughtful gift—like an illustrated picture book—to the person's home as congratulations.

Make it a recognition moment by including a handwritten note.

CARROT ACTION: In the front of the book, write the baby's name and a brief message, and sign your name. Take this one step further by recognizing the new grandpa or grandma.

Standing for Something

The consistent message.

If you are a leader or want to be a leader, you have to instill and inspire in people a sense of belief in what the company or team stands for. To gain the belief and loyalty of a group of people, there has to be a core set of principles, and you especially must be true to those ideals. There has to be consistency in your outlook and behavior. Otherwise, it's very hard to build a bond with your people.

The good news is, there are benefits of building a team with ideals. Such principles have been shown to drive enhanced team engagement, productivity, and camaraderie. Principles drive trust, and trust truly is a competitive advantage in business and in life. After all, there is a reason we trust brands such as Johnson & Johnson, Pepsi, American Express, and IBM—each of these companies tries its best to live up to high standards.

CARROT ACTION: Start by defining your principles and you'll end up enhancing the level of trust in your team. You'll be surprised at the results. Organizations with high trust levels spend considerably less recruiting new hires. Word of a positive culture spreads like wildfire.

Cultivating Action

Whistle while you work. Or work while you whistle.

People, much like crops, need nourishment and encouragement to grow. If we expect people to move faster, reach higher, and accomplish more, we need to be prepared to show our gratitude by providing others with the attention they deserve. If we want to build loyalty, we need to show loyalty. If we want respect, we need to show it. You scratch my back, I shave your back (you get the idea).

Recognition isn't a fancy new business policy. It's the law of nature. And so is communication, verbal and nonverbal. In most cases, we tell others what we expect from them through our own consistent action and results.

You can toss as many seeds as you want onto your front lawn, but if you don't tend to those seeds every day, they won't flourish.

CARROT ACTION: Try communicating today through actions alone. Roll up your sleeves, and get productive. Show those around you what you would normally tell them. Hit a deadline, make a sale, serve a customer.

The Gun Show

Titles don't make leaders. Actions do.

It's been documented that the late action film star Bruce Lee could perform fifty one-arm chin-ups. He weighed seventy-four pounds, but that's beside the point.

Lee's popularity on film was driven by his mystique off-screen—the numerous legends of his physical feats and extreme focus on the martial arts. It was his true ability, his tenaciousness, and determination to outdo himself, and his commitment to achieve what many perceived as impossible that made him a legend—not the fact that he was given the title of "movie star."

Titles don't create leaders. Leaders create titles.

CARROT ACTION: Reinvent your goals, focusing on achievements rather than titles. Instead of aiming to be appointed to the next "level," set your goals on performing and achieving the actions that will earn you the honor of reaching the next level.

Become a Student

Pay attention to great recognition ceremonies.

When you watch the Olympics or a Hollywood awards show on TV, take note of how they present their awards. Millions tune in to watch Olympians receive their medals; droves watch Oscar winners accept their awards. Anticipating and sharing the emotion of the moment is good watching. Likewise, our employees long for a little of that emotion in their recognition celebrations. So make it an event to remember.

CARROT ACTION: Study great recognition moments and model your award presentations after them, and you will soon become a master.

Initiative

How to make yourself more valuable.

So, your boss never praises you, and never acknowledges the great things you're accomplishing for the team. Unfortunately, we hear this complaint far too often. It's certainly easy to get angry about it or to start feeling sorry for yourself—to go home daily in a bad mood, full of righteous indignation, nurturing your animosity.

Snap out of it already. Take the initiative. Be the person who *does* acknowledge all the great work going on around you. When a co-worker accomplishes something, publicly recognize that person. Write thank-you cards to colleagues when they help you out. Let everyone know that you appreciate the great work they do for the team. No, you're not their boss, but you're a peer, and somebody has to take the first step.

CARROT ACTION: Here's your challenge today: write your boss a thank-you card for something that he or she did to help you. A Carrot Culture starts with small steps.

Consistency

Why reliability pays on a personal and corporate level.

It's clear that Walmart's success can be partially attributed to its fun marketing campaigns and low prices; but one of the core, underlying strengths of the Walmart brand rests in its consistency between locations. From Anchorage to Toledo, when you walk through the doors of a Walmart, you know that you're going to get consistently low prices and a wide selection.

Sam Walton, founder of the Walmart empire, was not only an honest and ethical man, but a person of consistency. Walton believed it was his duty to provide the lowest prices to his consumers. That was a core principle. And he stuck to his principles.

Consistency pays off personally, as well. First of all, because it's a rare virtue and you'll stand out at an individual and corporate level, and second, because people who demonstrate consistency are genuine. What you see is what you get. And that's a valuable and essential message to send.

CARROT ACTION: Work to gain ethical consistency and predictability. When you do, your life will demonstrate harmony between your values and your actions.

Count 'Em Up

*How many people we trust is often a good indication
of how trustworthy we are.*

Write down every person on this planet who you trust
implicitly and totally. Think carefully about this. Who
would you call first in a major crisis that required significant financial or emotional assistance? Who do you trust to
never take advantage of you—even when you are most vul-
nerable? Who would you trust to guide you through a challenging decision?

Now count them up.

It's amazing how small the number usually is. It's almost
never over fifty. Often it's as low as two, three, five, or ten,
which is to say that most of us are very careful in our judgment of whom we trust and whom we don't.

Trust breeds trust and those who do not easily trust others subconsciously understand that they are not trustworthy. That might not be completely true, but know that this
exercise has been used by ethics experts as a very simple
way to determine your own trustworthiness level.

CARROT ACTION: Look at your list. Are there any others you
have not thought of? Consider former teachers, friends, relatives, co-workers, and bosses. Keep trying to expand the list
and spread trust.

Live Fast

I figure the faster I pedal, the faster I can retire.
—Lance Armstrong

Recent studies have shown that the more career success people achieve in their twenties and early thirties, the greater their overall career growth curve will be later in life.

Does this mean that if you are over thirty it's too late to truly excel?

No, opportunity exists at any age, and that opportunity can often be manipulated by strategy. Put yourself in a place of opportunity today, and you're more likely to achieve your goals tomorrow.

CARROT ACTION: While setting your goals, define your place of opportunity. Are you where you need to be to learn about your goal, network with others who share your passion, and "get a foot in the door"?

Carrots for Kids

Be interested in others' families.

⌒⌒

You do something nice for me, I appreciate it. You do something nice for my family, and *we* are family.

Today, before you leave the office, ask each of your co-workers about his or her kids. Find out when their birthdays are and how old each child is. On your calendar, mark those dates and celebrate with them—whether through a birthday card or a handwritten note. A thoughtful picture book or toy given on the birthday of your co-worker's five-year-old daughter could be the best thing you've ever done for morale—and will certainly bring you closer to your team.

CARROT ACTION: Is it important to be close with your co-workers? Let's put it this way: Do you work harder for people you like and who like you, or those who seem aloof and superior?

Two Letter Impact

Get to yes.

At a sales training event in Dallas, a speaker motivates the crowd. "Get to yes!" he shouts. The audience, jam-packed with aggressive sales reps from various organizations, responds by screaming, "Yes!"

This shouting proceeds—growing louder and louder until everyone is in a frenzy of "yes-ness." As crazy as this tactic may sound, it seemed to work with these sales people. The speaker is basically instilling positive thinking and language into the minds of the attendees, not to mention raising the group's adrenaline.

Positive language influences people. Yet there is something just as impactful, if not more so, as the word "yes." It's the word "no." Sadly, we say it to ourselves and those around us too frequently. Instead of empowering us, it depletes us and those around us. Instead of motivating us, it stops us in our tracks. And, instead of raising our adrenaline, it shuts us off to the realm of possibility.

CARROT ACTION: Today, reframe your dialogue to arrive at "yes" answers. Remember, the word "no" closes conversations. The word "yes" opens negotiations.

Good People

Honest people are in demand in the workplace.

Ethical companies are looking for employees who understand that the ends do not justify the means. They want people who will voice concerns if something feels wrong, and to do everything in a legal manner—even the little things.

Many in accounting and human resource functions admit they'll look at expense reports before promoting someone. For example, does an employee record a business meal on an expense report when it is clear he or she is not traveling? It may seem petty, but if you can't be trusted with small dollars, it's hard to be trusted with decisions involving millions of dollars.

Honest people are in demand. Not surprising considering the worldwide brands and reputations that have been damaged and destroyed by individual bad apples.

CARROT ACTION: Realize that most leaders will hire and promote straight shooters who have a strong sense of personal integrity. Demonstrate an ability to be trusted in circumstances large and small.

For the Teacher

Thank the people who have influenced you.

We've all had at least one teacher who made a difference in our lives. Perhaps a motivating English teacher, a master of math, or a savvy shop instructor left a lasting impact. Send that dedicated educator a handwritten letter of thanks and explain, specifically, how he or she made a difference to you.

CARROT ACTION: Send a letter today to a teacher who made a difference in your life, or in the life of one of your children. Chances are your letter will be the best thing that happens to that teacher this week.

Fun and Games

Lighten up, will ya?

⌒⌒

This probably won't come as a surprise to you, but statistically the organizations that encourage a little fun at work see higher employee retention, satisfaction, and productivity.

Think about your all-time favorite boss. Did he or she ever enjoy a good laugh with you? Regale you now and then with a hilarious retelling of some event or mishap? Encourage an occasional game of foosball or ping-pong in the break room? They probably made you feel comfortable and loosened up.

Having an outlet for humor and fun is essential in a healthy, happy workplace. Break rooms with a card table, pool table, or video games are becoming commonplace for a reason. Tell an appropriate joke now and then, send along the occasional silly "dumb photo of the day," or just crack up your rigid face and shoot out a smile more often.

It's all part of building a lighter workplace. And even your smallest efforts can make a difference.

CARROT ACTION: Where possible, pick up the phone and, using your own voice, page yourself. Trust us, it's funny.

Your Secret Admirer

Someone thinks you're all that and a bag of chips.

Lois Lane was clueless when it came to Clark Kent. The guy had a huge crush on her, but her attention was always directed at Clark's alter ego—Superman. The relationship between Lois and Clark struck a nerve with fans—"If only she knew Clark could bench press a cruise ship!" they'd think.

All of us have people who admire us in life for various reasons. But, it's not too often that we stop to admire ourselves.

How do you become your own fan? It's simple—hold yourself accountable.

Recognize yourself when you meet your deadlines. Award yourself for taking the project to the next level. Applaud yourself for being honest or sharing your best ideas with the team.

CARROT ACTION: Create an award of self-accomplishment that you can wear, eat, or share with your team when you accomplish something great inside or outside of work. Let people, including yourself, be proud of their actions.

The Little Things

We underestimate the power of small acts of caring.

We know a fellow who keeps in his wallet a few short notes from his wife. He tells us that sometimes, when searching for a credit card, he'll stumble upon them.

"Or, on a really bad day at the office, I might purposely dig them out," he says.

No matter the occasion, reading them always puts him back on top of the world. A little thing, yes, but what an amazing impact.

The same thing goes for recognition at the office. It doesn't always have to be big, flashy, or expensive. A handwritten thank-you note, or a few words of praise in front of peers at a staff meeting. These small things can mean the world to your team members. And the simple memory of that recognition might be just what is needed to push a co-worker's performance over the top.

CARROT ACTION: Choose a small act of caring that you can undertake today.

Do a Trust Assessment

Asking for trust feedback takes courage,
but can enhance the way people see you.

Contact three people you know well, whether at work or in your personal life, and seek honest feedback. This will require courage. Let them know that you have made a conscious effort to increase your trustworthiness. Ask them to help you determine where you are trustworthy and where you are weak. Guarantee them that the candor with which they respond will not adversely affect your relationship, but will make it stronger. Keeping your promise to not become offended will be its own test of your trustworthiness.

How you are perceived by others is essential if you want to build your level of trustworthiness. Trust is established through action and over time, largely by keeping our word.

If you capture their comments in writing, you will get a great deal of your personal reputation in front of you, on paper, and categorized. And it was given to you by people whom you care about, and who are interested in helping you reach your goals. This is a valuable asset, and an important step in the right direction.

CARROT ACTION: You may ask for clarification during your conversations with others, but do not debate their comments.

Power Lift

*Our biggest achievements come while lifting
someone else into the spotlight.*
—Adrian Gostick and Chester Elton

There are two ways to reach your goals: (1) pulling everyone on your team along behind; or (2) pushing them out
front and letting them carry you to your ultimate destination.

Don't be afraid to build up your teammates or let them
shine. Every day you should find yourself publicly praising
your co-workers to others. It reflects well on you. And you'll
be surprised to find that there is room enough in the spotlight for your entire team.

CARROT ACTION: Out your team today. Find five ways to brag
about your teammates using electronic, written, and verbal
praise.

Just Listen

*Finding out what's going on around you
is a form of recognition.*

Give recognition today in a form other than "thank you."
Try *listening*.

Ask a co-worker about his weekend, and then *listen* to
his response. You'll probably learn something about him
that you didn't know. And he'll feel good that you cared
enough to ask.

When your kids get home from school, rather than nag-
ging about homework or the dishes, start their afternoon by
asking, "What was crazy at school today?" And then *listen*.
You might find out something about your kid or his friends
that you didn't know, and you'll strengthen your relationship.

When you're with your friends, instead of complaining
about your job or bragging about your kids, ask a friend
about her job or her kids and then *listen*. She'll be thrilled
to have a friend who actually listens and cares.

CARROT ACTION: Just for today, forget about the minutiae
going on in your life and find out what's up with others. Your
co-workers will appreciate that you care enough to ask and
listen. Remember, people won't necessarily remember what
you say, but they will always remember how you make them
feel.

Sorry. No time.

How much time does it take to say thanks?

We all are busy. But acts of recognition should not take an inordinate amount of your time. The most successful people we've studied take time out to recognize co-workers and employees because it leads to higher productivity, better workplaces, and, as corny as it sounds, it really *is* the right thing to do.

To quantify this, those people were not spending more than an hour a week on recognition. That's only about two percent of their time, but it was time that was paying off in big ways.

CARROT ACTION: Spend an hour this week on recognition activities and on Friday review the results. Plan for the following week accordingly.

Pants on Fire

"A lie cannot live."
—Dr. Martin Luther King, Jr.

⌐⌐

Honesty is sometimes the most difficult demand we can place on ourselves—especially when a little, itty-bitty lie could possibly save us from headache, or grant us a small reward.

A cab driver, not too long ago, picked us up outside a hotel lobby. Without too much conversation we hopped in and headed to our destination. Along the way we asked, "What's your rate to the airport?"

The cab driver glanced in the rearview mirror and asked, "Have you been to this city before?"

"Sure," we replied. "We could show you the way."

His facial expressions spoke volumes when he responded, "Well, then it's twelve dollars." We give away more than we know when we lie. Never get to the point where you must be forced to tell the truth.

CARROT ACTION: Share the full truth today with everyone you talk to, even if the truth hurts. You'll build trust.

Applaud Them for Messing Up

*Give yourself and others permission
to recover from a mistake.*

Who hasn't messed up royally at work? As an employee, it's hard to admit when you've made a mistake. If you are a manager, try recognizing your employees when they tell you about a mistake, before it becomes a whopper.

One leader we met has a box of small action figures by his desk. When an employee admits a mistake, he hands them Batman and tells them they are a hero for trying. Giving the figure is a way to break the ice and make the mistake less embarrassing. The manager says that this action figure ritual makes employees admit small mistakes right when they're made, instead of later, when the mistake has become a colossal problem. Better still, the action figures have also become rewards for honesty.

This tactic has created trust among employees and their manager, and, as a department, they now report the smallest amount of losses from mistakes in their company—because they catch them early.

CARROT ACTION: Come up with your team's "Mistake Award" right now. Make it fun, silly, and politically correct!

Herd Mentality

Your attitude is your responsibility.

It oozes, gushes, and seeps into every corner of our lives. It's a mess—contagious as a media story on the latest flu outbreak. It breeds fear, mistrust, low productivity, hostility, and even physical illness (well, at least it makes people use their sick days).

What is it? It's a negative attitude. But, what came first? Toxic employees or a toxic culture?

Where it came from, and who's to blame, doesn't really matter. The only thing that matters is finding a cure—and that starts with you. You're accountable for your attitude.

The good news here is that a positive attitude can be just as contagious as any flu.

CARROT ACTION: Today, when you're approached by someone with a bad attitude, stop the negativity in its tracks. Respond to the gossip, the complaining, and groaning by saying, "You know what, I'm actually excited about today. There's a lot of great stuff going on here. I hope your day gets better!"

While You're Out

Recognition can happen, even when you're miles away.

⌐⌐

When you are out of the office, there is most likely is a colleague who fills in for you. One man we talked with at a manufacturing company found a way to thank his co-worker when he was on the road.

"We were a staff of six a few years ago. Now, with the declining economy, there are only two of us left. So, it's more important than ever to recognize," he said. "With my co-worker, I understand her as an individual. For example, a simple thing, but she loves getting a chocolate chip cookie from the cafeteria every morning."

So when the man went on a week-long business trip, he left her $5—enough to buy a fresh-baked cookie from the cafeteria each day. Said the man, "She's stuck in the office, picking up the slack, while I'm traveling, so I want to make sure that every day some recognition is happening."

CARROT ACTION: Is there someone you can identify who has helped fill in for you while you were traveling or on vacation? What personalized recognition can you give them today? Keep this up every time you are away from the office.

Give Back

Take Albert's advice.

Albert Einstein said that from the standpoint of daily living, there is one thing we do know, that we are here for the sake of each other.

"Above all for those upon whose smile and well being our own happiness depends, and also for those countless unknown souls with whose fate we are connected by a bond of sympathy. Many times a day I realize how much my own outer and inner life is built upon the labors of my fellow man, both living and dead, and how earnestly I must exert myself in order to give in return as much as I have received."

CARROT ACTION: When you feel like the world is closing in on you and nothing is going right, take a tip from the guy that came up with the theory of relativity—count your blessings and be grateful for all the people who love and support you, and make the conscious decision to give back.

Own Your Mistakes

Take control.

In any organization trust is built on honest, open communication in good times and especially in bad. When mistakes are made in a trusting environment, resources can be rallied—turning mistakes into opportunities to recover and make things right for a client or co-worker. One example that struck us happened in the 1980s in Detroit. Chrysler executives were driving vehicles, and then someone within the company decided it was a good idea to turn back the odometer and sell them as new.

When this was discovered, you can only imagine what was happening within the organization. The legal counsel was most likely advising, "You must deny this, you must spin this." In doing the right thing, Lee Iacocca took out a full page ad in the *Detroit Free Press* and admitted his company had made a mistake. He said they had breached the trust and integrity of their customers. They acknowledged this and promised it would never happen again. And Chrysler survived the crisis. Why? Because they did the right thing quickly.

CARROT ACTION: Next time you make a mistake, and you will, get out in front of the problem as soon as you can. Own your mistakes and offer a way to correct the problem.

And Then What?

If I'd had some set idea of a finish line,
don't you think I would have crossed it years ago?
—Bill Gates

The irony of success is that the moment you stop succeeding you become a failure—history is erased, achievements are marginalized. This sentence might seem awfully pessimistic, but you could look at it the way Bill Gates does; the achievement of one goal gives you the opportunity to set more goals and achieve greater accomplishments.

One of the biggest reasons people report not setting goals is that, "there's no way to predict the future." And, as much as that statement is true, it's the consistent ritual of setting goals that makes success itself a ritual.

CARROT ACTION: Set your daily goals first, weekly goals second, and monthly goals third. Now double your monthly goal and multiply it by twelve—plan for a whole year. Now we're talking optimistic.

First Person

A warm reception.

Surprise your department's administrative assistant with doughnuts, flowers, a fruit basket, or a simple thank-you card and watch as that person's area becomes brighter and friendlier.

Chances are few people on your team formally thank this talented individual—the person who most customers view as the face of your company.

CARROT ACTION: Do it today. Give something that she/he can keep for a few days.

Allow Celebration

Make the "Big Talkers" talk for you.

One woman told us, "I wish we didn't have to tell the boss about our big win." Another co-worker laughed and said, "I know, we'll have to listen to him tell us that it's nothing compared to what he used to do."

Many of us have had a manager or friend who is always looking to belittle our performance. In business and in life, competition can be fierce—even when we think we're not competing.

Give power to receive power in return. Compliment first. Recognize first. Reward and celebrate others before yourself, and you'll be shocked by how much celebration is reciprocated from the people you expect it from least.

CARROT ACTION: Find the big talker today. Become her biggest fan. Soon, she'll be talking big about you!

Use Your Customers' Products

Let them eat cupcake.

Does one of your clients or customers produce a product that you could use as an award? If so, order some for your next recognition event. We consulted with the folks at Sara Lee and used their snack foods as a team "thank you." People loved it.

The benefits of this approach are twofold: your employees get the recognition they deserve—along with a subtle reminder of the importance of your valued clients. And your clients will be pleased to know that you like their products enough to use them as awards.

Carrot Action: Find a client product today. If your client is BMW, you are going to be one popular person.

You're Fired

*Show me a person who doesn't get fired
with enthusiasm, and I'll show you a person
who gets fired, with enthusiasm.*
—Vince Lombardi

The chairman and chief executive officer of a large financial institution recently received a lot of media attention—most calling foul on the man—who, while his company was attempting to mend economic struggles, allegedly purchased an $87,000 rug for his office. (It may have driven the company further into debt, but it did go nicely with his Fabergé egg collection.)

Before the incidents that led to the CEO's departure, he had a seemingly unblemished reputation. So, many were asking, what happened?

Accountability is not something that can be given—it must be taken. All too often we are given accountability—diluting our enthusiasm, our passion, and our drive to own responsibility for our actions.

CARROT ACTION: Analyze those things to which you hold yourself accountable. If your list includes responsibilities that don't drive your enthusiasm, learn to delegate.

Works of the Hand

The more personal, the more valued.

At the Morgan Library in New York City you can view a remarkable collection of rare manuscripts and first edition books. It is a moving experience to get so close to a letter signed by T. S. Eliot (with his dramatic capital T) or an original Beethoven composition and his countless reworking scratch marks.

These works of the hand are priceless because they show the artist's hand. The creator crafted each work in a very personal way.

The advent of the digital age has made handwritten works more rare, and therefore even more valuable. And yet the art of letter writing and the courtesy of a handwritten thank-you note are going the way of the dodo—despite the very personal impact they have on recipients.

CARROT ACTION: Take the time to make your next thank you personal. Make it a work of your hand. Years from now it may end up in a museum. At the very least, it won't be deleted seconds after being received.

A High-Trust Environment

*Take time to evaluate the moral well-being
of your organization.*

Want to enhance your trustworthiness? Work at a morally grounded organization. Ask yourself the following:

1. Is there an unreasonably high focus on the company stock price, as opposed to creating long-term value for shareholders?
2. Is company communication frequent and open, or are things communicated on a "need-to-know" basis?
3. Is it okay to admit you've made a mistake? Can you recall a supervisor publicly admitting an error?
4. Have you ever been asked to violate your personal ethical standards (i.e., erasing emails, misrepresenting company services or profits, lying to an outside party, etc.)?
5. Do you trust your immediate supervisors? How about upper management?
6. Are you proud to tell your friends and family where you work?

If your organization, based on this quiz, isn't truthworthy, you have two choices: Work to change the environment or get out of Dodge.

CARROT ACTION: Evaluate your environment today and put together a plan to enhance the level of trustworthiness.

Clarity or Disparity?

Instant connections or irritating quirks?

Karen was a "work hugger." She hugged co-workers, customers, and vendors. Phil, on the other hand, hated to be hugged. He liked working with Karen, but he was uncomfortable when she, or anyone, touched him.

So, who's the weird one? Karen or Phil?

Everyone will answer that question differently depending on his preferred communication style, culture, and upbringing. Some people communicate through touch, others mostly through words, and some by hand gestures and visual descriptions.

If you want to understand how someone will best understand your message, observe how they communicate.

CARROT ACTION: Note today how communication styles can greatly impact the way an employee or co-worker responds to recognition or criticism. Take care to observe the specific styles of all of your co-workers.

Some Things Never Change

Real change requires effort and momentum—from you.

If you're like most people, you've come up with a long list of things you'd like to change by this point in the book. That's great. It shows you're thinking about your character. But don't try to do them all at once.

Instead, for one week, pick just *two*. One should be something you will do differently. The other should be something you won't do anymore. For example, a list might look like:

1. I *will* use specific language to thank my colleagues when they help me with my assignments.
2. I *won't* miss deadlines or be untrue to my word.

Try to choose actions that will apply to situations that occur *frequently*. Keep each goal *manageable* so that you can succeed. Also, choose goals that are *specific*, not general. For example, a goal like, "I won't lie at work," is harder to fulfill than one that specifies, "I won't lie on my time card," or "I won't use sick days when I'm not sick." These should get progressively harder as you continue to improve.

CARROT ACTION: Concentrate on these goals for one week, then choose two more. Work on those, as you continue to master these behaviors.

Surround Yourself with Ethical Friends

The law of reciprocity: you'll only be trusted as you trust others.

Do people you consider friends cheat on their taxes and brag about it, or steal from their employers? In your family, do you support your children in lying to their teachers about tardiness or absences? Trust is just as critical in these relationships as it is in your work relationships.

How many marriages do you know that have been successful without partners trusting each other? The sad fact is that very few marriages survive without trust. Marriage is built on it. Friendships are built on trust. Business relationships are built on trust.

CARROT ACTION: The first step in building trusting relationships is to extend trust to others. Evaluate your personal relationships to determine where you need to trust more.

. . . Must Come Down

*Everyone sooner or later sits down
to a banquet of consequences.*
—Robert Louis Stevenson

The simple meaning of the word consequence is: something that happens as a result of an action. It's an unbiased definition—it doesn't judge whether the actions taken were noble or mischievous, or whether the results of those actions were positive or negative.

Consequences are simply the result of every action.

A funky haircut may intrigue one person, while creating separation with others. Attitudes may create friends, or initiate a posse of enemies. Scratching an itch provides instant gratification, but still breaks the outermost layer of the skin. And, even lackluster work performance may be viewed by one manager as pathetic, yet viewed by another as, "at least they don't try to outshine me."

For everything there is a consequence—good or bad. The good news is you can anticipate one or the other.

CARROT ACTION: Learn to appreciate consequences and the analysis of how your consequences arrived. Learn from the bad. Improve on the good.

Run Forrest, Run

Hone those instincts.

⌒

Sea turtles hatched on a beach instinctually move toward the ocean. They receive no training from their mother, and have no experiential data on which to base their actions. There's no sign saying sea, this way.

Instinct is innate—in animals and humans. And until we learn to fear our natural inclinations, or respond to variables in our life based on past experience, our instincts pull us naturally in certain directions.

Imagine what would happen if a sea turtle, before reaching the sea, was told that the ocean was a dangerous place, and the risk should be avoided. And imagine if the young turtle listened to that advice, staying exactly where he was, refusing to ever respond to his natural urge to swim. There wouldn't be very many sea turtles left.

How many of us ignore our instincts, our natural abilities, and our innate strengths? Why? Do you really have a reason that excuses you from a life's calling?

Swim little turtle, swim.

CARROT ACTION: Help a friend define his or her innate abilities today.

Accomplish a Goal— for Someone Else

Enough about you; help someone else succeed.

⌒⌒

Ever had a goal that you needed help to accomplish? Have you ever had someone else offer to help you accomplish a goal? Here's an idea: be that person!

It may be helping a colleague get a promotion by writing him a letter of recommendation, or lending a hand to the would-be Eagle Scout's efforts to gather used books for the local children's hospital, or supporting a friend in her goal to lose weight by hiking alongside her. Helping someone reach her goal—whatever it is—shows that you're interested in her and want her to succeed.

CARROT ACTION: Rather than ignoring or even hindering someone's attempt at reaching a goal, help him accomplish it. Ask what you can do to help, and then do it. The Carrot you're giving might not even be the "help"—it could be just the fact that you've shown confidence in his abilities. And that confidence might just be the momentum he needs to achieve his goal!

Bite Off More

How big is your plate of possibility?

Serving sizes in the United States continue to grow. Today, the average French fry serving size is nearly four times larger what is was just twenty years ago. Single size drinks, sometimes sixty-four ounces, may be the size of a carton of milk. Today, our side dishes are bigger than our main courses.

While it's not good for our health, this supersizing concept is great when it comes to our potential. Why do we limit ourselves when it comes to our potential—and goal setting?

Instead, supersize your goals—make them bigger than your reality. Roll up your sleeves, and get ravenous with motivation.

CARROT ACTION: Today look at your list of goals. Which goal could you supersize, making it a true stretch goal?

No Such Thing as a Free Lunch

The power of listening over soup.

~~

If you are a leader at work, every two or three weeks, emerge from your fortress—aka your office—and invite three to five of your employees to lunch. Tell them that you'll pay the tab if they come with a concern or problem and a viable solution for it.

It's a perfect way to recognize your people. They get the chance to eat for free, with the boss listening directly to them. You get something out of it too: access to their opinions, concerns, solutions, and ideas.

This gives you time to actually listen to those around you—you may be shocked at the information you get. They may bring a concern to your attention that you didn't even realize was a problem. They may have solutions that are unique and practical. You may discover untapped talent in an employee.

Obviously the conversation will stray from business, so this is an opportunity to learn more about your employees personally, as well.

CARROT ACTION: Start today. If you haven't eaten yet, invite three of your employees to join you and see what a difference it makes in your day.

Think Small

Break it down.

There's a very good chance that this page will be read in its entirety because it's the one of the shortest entries in the book. It's so short that nobody will turn the page claiming that they don't have time to read it.

The point is brief, too: breaking big concepts into small segments creates easily manageable progress.

CARROT ACTION: Grab the project you've been hiding and dedicate ten minutes of your day to it. Just ten minutes. Simply define the very first step. Tomorrow, dedicate fifteen minutes to successfully beginning that first step. Don't think about any other steps until the first step is complete.

Homeward Bound

Recognize their family.

⌐⌐

We were in Michigan one gray winter day, speaking to the leadership team of an automotive supply company. At one point, a vice president told us her team was working harder than ever in this tough economy, so she had begun recognizing the families of employees.

For example, she said, "Recently I had an employee who had to work late for several weeks straight to put in a new software system. It was hard work, and I appreciated his great work. At the end of the period, on a Friday afternoon, I sent his wife flowers and a note of thanks."

When the employee showed up for work on Monday morning, she asked, "So, did your wife get the flowers?" He nodded. "Yep. Now she wants me to work even harder for you."

CARROT ACTION: Recognize the families or partners of your co-workers for their sacrifices. It's undoubtedly one of the most powerful (and largely untapped) motivational tools we have ever seen.

Build, Don't Tear Down

Better the lives of others.

If you had to list five things that are going wrong in your office right now, what would they be? Simple, right?

Now, list five things that are right on track. Stumped?

It's always easier to find fault than to build up. Master builders devote years to structures that can be destroyed in minutes by vandals and looters. Your people are much the same.

When you honor someone's contributions in front of their peers in a dignified way you *build* people. When you criticize them in front of their peers you *destroy* them.

Use recognition liberally and your criticism sparingly. Trust and confidence are built over time and with great care. Recognition moments can help you build solid and valuable relationships.

CARROT ACTION: Take care to reserve sharp comments and criticism for one-on-one meetings. Recognition is public; criticism is private.

Hindsight vs. Foresight

*To be what we are, and to become what we are
capable of becoming, is the only end in life.*
—Robert Louis Stevenson

There's an old saying: "hindsight is 20/20." But does the past dictate the future?

Born to working-class parents, one young boy learned the value of a strong work ethic at an early age. To help make ends meet he and his brothers and sisters were expected to work in a factory—eight hours a day while also attending school. Still, it wasn't enough to save the family home. Eventually, the family was forced into living out of a camper van.

Without an address, it's hard to find a job. Without money, it's hard to fund an education. And with little support, and no direct role models, it's hard to envision a dream, especially when your dream is to become a stand-up comedian.

Nevertheless, Jim Carrey decided he'd had enough of his negative history and took a shot at his future. He began performing celebrity impressions at small clubs. His passion drove him. His talent carried him. And his future is now comedic history.

CARROT ACTION: What doesn't the world expect from you? Is it your passion? Make a commitment to stepping out on your stage for the first time.

Give Your Company a Trust Exam

If you are surrounded by morally ill people,
it can be hard to be trustworthy yourself.

Use your eyes, ears, and cerebellum to help you understand the trust level of your company and your team. What have you experienced? Filed away in your mind are clear pictures of company decisions and the processes used to reach those decisions. Hopefully, your evaluation will reveal an organization that values trust and has a consistent system to reward and reinforce it.

What if you find yourself in an organization with the philosophy that we might describe as, "do whatever it takes, look the other way, we've got to make our numbers"? That's when it's time to decide if you can improve the situation, compromise, or move on. And people with integrity never compromise their ethics.

CARROT ACTION: Work isn't the only organization to which you belong. Most of us belong to many—family, social, sporting, religious, political, and so on. Evaluate these organizations as you did your work.

Punch Up Engagement

Care enough to give the gift of a good bout.

We met a businesswoman who was frustrated. She was working on a project that was creating a lot of aggravation for her, which the rest of her team. Morale, engagement, and productivity were all suffering.

Her co-worker, Dave, didn't wait for the boss to do something, but gathered the team on his own. He expressed admiration for their co-worker's extra efforts on the project and acknowledged her frustrations. Then he presented her with a punching bag that she could place on her desk to punch out her irritation.

The woman grabbed the bag and immediately started punching. The result was better than anyone could have expected. The entire team, and even the boss, took turns punching the bag. People laughed and relaxed; the alleviation of stress was palpable.

All this from a punching bag? Of course not. Some of it was because this woman's co-worker had been paying attention and thanked her for doing a great job despite the hurdles she'd been experiencing.

CARROT ACTION: What are your co-workers working on? What frustrations are they dealing with? They'll be flattered that you care enough to find out. Go a step further and find them some kind of punching bag or stress doll to help them— and the rest of your team—relax.

Formal Awards

Presentation is (almost) everything.

Most formal awards—for years of service or above-and-beyond achievement—are presented without much fanfare. But according to a survey we conducted with thirty thousand award recipients, how you present an award makes a significant impression. In fact, 97 percent of employees felt their "contributions were acknowledged" after an "excellent" award presentation. Only 39 percent of people felt their contributions were acknowledged after a "poor" presentation or no presentation.

To ensure sincerity and meaning, two or three co-workers should make comments. These should be people who personally know the recipient and can shed light on his achievements to others. Encourage them to make only positive, upbeat comments—focusing on the very best things that are happening in your workplace and how the recipient fits into those achievements.

CARROT ACTION: Before the next formal award presentation in your department, make some notes of exactly what is being recognized and be prepared to talk about the employee's specific contributions that have affected the company.

Wandering Eyes, Wondering Why

Are you speaking to an auditory communicator?

"Ugh, that guy in distribution just doesn't listen when I talk to him. He's rude—actually turning to look off into the distance when I give him instructions."

If you haven't noticed yet, not everyone communicates in the same fashion. Auditory communicators can be recognized by the distance they keep in conversation, and a tendency to turn one of their ears to the conversation rather than their eyes. Auditory communicators remember words spoken and inflection used during the conversation.

Don't be mistaken; just because they don't make eye contact doesn't mean auditory communicators are rude—rather, they are likely hearing every detail and remembering every word. They are listening intently.

There are, of course, actual rude people who truly don't listen, but that's another story.

CARROT ACTION: Understand the communication styles of the people close to you. It will help you communicate more effectively with them.

The Uncomfortable Stare

Are you speaking to a visual communicator?

"Janice freaks me out. She glares at me—right into my eyes—like she's boring into my head. I feel like I've done something wrong."

Ladies and gents, don't be alarmed, Janice is a visual communicator. Visual communicators can be recognized by their direct eye contact, their attention to detail, and their descriptive language. Visual communicators will explain "how things look." In conversations they feel most comfortable when they can see expressions, and typically are very conscious about appearance and what that appearance communicates.

Don't be mistaken, visual communicators aren't flirting or trying to intimidate you. They simply communicate via what they see and what they show.

CARROT ACTION: Join the language of your conversational counterpart—even if it's just for a brief period. Matching a person's communication style builds trust.

Touch and Feel

Are you speaking to a kinesthetic communicator?

"Ronnie is an odd duck. Why does he insist on swatting me on the back every time he walks by me in the hallway? And why is he so sensitive?"

Feelings, touch, taste, and smell coming into play? You must be talking to a kinesthetic communicator. They can be recognized by their closeness during conversation, frequent touching, and descriptions of "how things felt." Kinesthetic communicators are good at picking up "vibes" or sensing the feelings of others. They are highly sensitive to their surroundings, and the way others communicate toward them.

Want the best hug in town? Find a kinesthetic.

CARROT ACTION: Shake someone's hand today. It says a lot without saying anything at all.

Bad Odor

Do you want someone to tell you?

Walk into any office in the world where employees are unhappy about their working conditions, their managers, or the company policies and you'll hear some pretty nasty statements. Walk into a managers' meeting and you'll hear complaints about employees—their engagement, work skills, and their performance.

If everybody stinks, why isn't anyone willing to speak up?

Breaking the silence, sharing frustrations, and communicating freely are the only true means of resolving differences and reaching common ground.

CARROT ACTION: Research shows that a mixture of positive praise with criticism is crucial to human development. However, the research also shows that the greatest development happens when each criticism is followed or preceded by five positive statements.

Who's on first?

Turn an obstacle into an opportunity.

Lou Costello was driven to learn and master the art of comedic timing, character, and pacing, in his attempt to present a clean show in often raunchy venues, the places where most comedians were finding work in the 1920s and '30s. Like many comedians of the time, Costello typically worked with a straight man, a person who would set up the joke, and rein in the comedian if he was starting to lose the audience.

One night in 1931, Costello's normal straight man canceled at the last minute. Costello knew he couldn't pull off the show on his own, so he asked the theater manager to fill in. Bud Abbott agreed. That night, the birth of one of the greatest comedy teams of all time happened unexpectedly.

Goals, when set properly, do not disappear behind hurdles. Lou Costello was bound and determined to reach his goal and because of it, he bumped into his future.

CARROT ACTION: Make a list of the people you believe are necessary to completing your goal. Now, pretend that all of them have disappeared. Create a plan to continue the journey.

The Team Player

*No one is useless in this world who lightens
the burdens for anyone else.*
—Charles Dickens

Great work is about teamwork; it happens when everyone is willing to pitch in, roll up their proverbial sleeves, and do whatever it takes to succeed. As you rub shoulders with your co-workers, joining them in their struggle, your great example will start to rub off on them and everything will get easier.

One employee we spoke with says if his co-workers don't get an assignment done that day, he says, "Don't worry, I'll stay late and do it for you." He says that subtle challenge motivates most people to beat him to the punch.

CARROT ACTION: How can you lighten the load for someone on your team today?

Fun and Games

You got the music in you.

⌒

One of Microsoft's many divisions once told us that every day they enjoy a game of "three o'clock rock." Every afternoon at three it's someone's turn to select a song from their vast digital collection and crank it up for all to hear. Teammates know that if they've got a phone call, they need to wrap it up by then to enjoy the quick music break. They stand up, sing along, laugh, and relax while getting a glimpse into the personality of the song selector.

Other office teams employ the same idea but rather than turn up the speakers, the "DJ" simply sends a link to the song to everyone to listen to or comment on via live chatting or email. Playful e-banter ensues and after a few minutes people return to their tasks refreshed and refocused.

Another variation is to play a quick round of "Name That Tune" where that day's person plays five or six introductions to various songs on the speakers until the others correctly guess the song and artist.

CARROT ACTION: Try it this afternoon. Find a song from the past, turn up your speakers, and ask if anyone remembers it.

Blindfolded

There is not a right way to do a wrong thing.

Jim Duncan had a plan for his ad agency. It included implementing new processes and procedures to complete projects faster and acquire new clients faster.

Jim purchased task-management software. He drew detailed charts. He typed detailed processes. He required all employees to train extensively in the new system.

But he never explained—much less defined for himself—the *goal* of the new strategy to his team.

Goal setting is about creating a clear objective. After that's defined, you can begin to shape the process, develop a plan, and get others on board.

CARROT ACTION: Move backward today. Start as if your goal was already accomplished and design your processes in reverse.

It's Not You, It's Me

You complete me.
—Jerry Maguire

Many of us would love to be in a relationship, if we could only find the perfect partner. We would love to be passionate employees, if management wasn't so dim-witted. We'd even be role models if the kids these days weren't so bad to the bone.

Sense the sarcasm? All of the above statements are limiting assumptions we tend to make in life to avoid accountability for our own imperfections. Sure, there are plenty of people to blame in this world—many of whom deserve blame—but, where is blame going to get us if we cannot blame ourselves? It's important to remember that our imperfections are the only imperfections we can control and change.

CARROT ACTION: Today, make yourself the focus of blame. Sometimes knowing and acknowledging where we are weak will show us where we are strong and how we can grow stronger.

We Got the Beat

How rhythm and timing are critical to communication.

"There's nothing more irritating than a person who drops long pauses between their words or thoughts."

Or:

"There's nothing more irritating than someone who can't enjoy silence—constantly talking to fill any gaps."

We all have different opinions. And, we all have different rhythms that we respond to. The goal is to get everyone on the same musical sheet, so that each beat can complement the others.

CARROT ACTION: Create an office-supplies orchestra with your team today (this can even be done without the boss's knowledge from behind your cubicle walls). Allow each team member to play a different instrument—stapler, phone, paperclip box. It sounds silly, but it's a great exercise in teamwork and communication, and active listening.

Teach 'Why,' Not 'How'

Education is not the filling of a pail,
but the lighting of a fire.
—William Butler Yeats

Ava, an eight-year-old living in Arizona, begged for a puppy. Her parents weighed the pros and cons of the decision heavily—finally agreeing that it might teach their daughter how to be responsible.

Of course, this meant that Ava was responsible for "poop-scooping" in the back yard. Her father showed her how to do it. Her mother told her when to do it—daily.

At first, Ava was thrilled to run in the back with the puppy, a Golden Retriever. But, as the dog quickly grew, so did the task at hand. Soon, Ava whined about her responsibility.

Her parents insisted that her chore be completed daily, until one day, Ava asked, "Why do I have to do it every day?"

Her parents surrendered. Of course, the very next day, the puppy came romping through the house, tracking in . . .

"That's why," Ava's parents said. "Now you have to clean the mess."

CARROT ACTION: When giving instruction, teach people why their responsibilities are important. True accountability occurs when people understand the whole picture.

Recognition Rut?

It takes creative thinking to come up with new ideas.

In a recognition rut? Try recognizing your co-workers and employees in creative ways that don't include a tangible item or even a public presentation.

For example, when our employee Andrea had been with our firm for only seven months, we asked her to walk the CEO of our parent company through a new training offering.

At first, Andrea admitted that she thought she was in trouble or was being given an unpleasant task that we didn't want to do. But as she began preparing for the presentation, she became increasingly excited about the opportunity. "I was being given the chance to meet with the CEO face to face—how many new employees get to do that?" she said.

For Andrea, the presentation proved to be a great way to recognize her. We wanted to show her off, and we wanted her to present the material to our CEO in an articulate manner. Both goals were accomplished, and Andrea knew how much she was valued.

CARROT ACTION: What motivates your colleagues? Don't know? Find out. That's the key to getting out of the recognition rut!

I Trust You

Sometimes you offer a carrot when you ask for help.

Sometimes the best recognition isn't "thank you," but, "I trust you." Are you the person on your team who hoards plum assignments? You don't delegate or ask for help because you want to make sure the job is done exactly how you want it done? Maybe, if you are to be honest, you might admit that you're afraid that one of your co-workers *is* capable of doing the job and might actually do it better than you.

If this is true in your case, quit being a control freak and glory hound and let your co-workers help. In most cases, they'll be honored that you asked. The fact that you're asking for help is just another way of saying, "I trust you." Your co-workers will love that carrot, and the team will be stronger because of it.

CARROT ACTION: Ask for advice or help on just one task today. Your teammate will realize that you trust her and her abilities enough to help, and you are reshaping yourself at the same time.

Stress Reduction

This reward really hits the spot.

We all know how much damage stress can cause in the workplace. For a team reward, bring in a massage therapist and chair for a day. Your team will not only feel appreciated, they'll be healthier. It'll be a day they will remember, and work hard to make happen again.

If massage is awkward, try meditation or yoga instead.

CARROT ACTION: Ahhh.

Rock and a Hard Place

Do or do not. There is no try.
—Yoda

Aron Ralston was stuck in situation that needed a decision.

While hiking in a canyon the young man got his arm stuck underneath a boulder. If he stayed, he'd die. After five days alone, he realized his only way out was to cut off his lower arm with a pocket knife.

In those crucial moments, the word "try" did not exist. He wasn't going to start and stop, although he knew his actions could potentially be just as dangerous as waiting for someone to find him.

We don't always know what the ultimate results of our decisions will be, but we cannot always allow that to stop us from taking steps toward a goal.

Embarking on a path to a goal isn't something to be "tried." It is something to be done. Eliminate the word "try" from your vocabulary.

CARROT ACTION: Dedicate yourself to your goal by finally accepting the sacrifices that have held you back.

Make Someone Great

I resemble that remark.
—Curly Howard

What if other people were like putty in your hands? What if you could simply mold their workplace behaviors and priorities to match your highest expectations?

In a way, you can. Each time we praise people, they further develop the recognized abilities. Be frequent in your praise, be specific in relating what matters most to your team's goals, and finally be timely.

CARROT ACTION: Praise someone today for meeting deadlines. They'll be early next time. Did you ever imagine you had such power? Go ahead, make someone great today.

Lighten Up, Dude

Great men are rarely isolated mountain peaks;
they are the summits of ranges.
—Thomas W. Higginson

Work is serious business. Life is serious business. Relationships are serious business.

So, why do we hamper their potential by limiting ourselves to only serious conversations? Everyone has at least a *sense* of humor, though some are loathe to face up to it.

Effective communication happens when conversations are real, honest, and yes, even funny. Effective communication is when we speak from the heart, think from the head, and laugh from the belly.

Humor can be one way to get your point across effectively.

CARROT ACTION: Prove a point today by sharing a funny story with your team, or your loved ones. Your audience will listen more intently because its defenses are down, and its interest is up.

From the President

Create a red-letter day.

⌐⌐

We all want to know that someone in a position of authority knows we add value. Ask your company president, managing director, or other highest ranking official to write a letter of thanks to a team member who has put forth his very best effort and then some. It's one letter that, most likely, will be kept forever.

CARROT ACTION: If the president is too busy to write a letter, let him know that an email is an option.

Make Your Boss Look Good

Toss the boss a carrot.

When was the last time you made your boss look good? There's no better carrot for your boss than the knowledge that she hired the right person. And that confirmation comes with your success.

When you succeed or fail, it's a direct reflection on your boss. So step up to the plate, go above and beyond—don't just be a "paycheck" employee. Your efforts and hard work will be noticed; your boss will appreciate you more than she can say because you're making her look like a recruiting genius. She looks brilliant in the eyes of *her* boss—and that is priceless. This is when your stock starts going up and you become an invaluable asset to the team and the company.

CARROT ACTION: Anticipate your boss's needs. Is there a special report or project that she would like you to get started on? Then take the initiative. She'll appreciate your proactive approach. It's a great first step towards making her look good.

Lose the "Good Job"

When it's specific, praise is effective.

⌒⌒

At one of California's largest theme parks (run by man-sized rodents) managers are told to avoid generic praise like: "Good job." Officials there have discovered that general praise can actually have a negative impact on employees.

Imagine that you've been working hard all day, making sure rides are running smoothly, guests are safe, and people are happy. You are hot. You're hungry. And about fifteen kids in a row have rubbed cotton candy on your uniform. But, hey, you're still smiling.

Then, a colleague or a manager wanders by for the first time that day and fires off a glib, "Hey, Stevie. Keep up the good work." Your response (muttered under your breath, of course): "That bozo has no idea what I've been doing."

Compare that with someone who is watching your good work. Perhaps she comments, "Steve, I was really impressed with how you handled the guests at your ride during that break for maintenance. The folks seemed a little put out, but your positive attitude kept them smiling. Thanks so much."

CARROT ACTION: Try it right now. Gather some colleagues together and give specific praise to a team member. Watch the reaction.

Extra Crispy or Original?

Goals are engineered like buildings—
an idea becomes a model, and models become reality.

Harlan Sanders was a café and motel owner who lived in Kentucky. His recipes were applauded, especially the one for his fried chicken. But Harlan couldn't sell very much chicken because it took thirty minutes to cook.

Enter the pressure cooker, also known to us as the deep fryer.

This story goes exactly where you think it will. Sanders built one of the world's most recognized and iconic franchises.

Don't get us wrong, KFC is irresistible, with the secret recipe that took years to perfect. But the company's success is really due to the fact that Colonel Sanders had a scalable goal—grow his business with good partners, one restaurant at time, repeating the same system over and over.

The same rules apply to your goal. Take one small aspect of your goal, perfect it, and repeat. Also keep in mind that it never hurts to find good partners, just like Sanders did.

CARROT ACTION: Make your life scalable—because it's not always going to be the same size as it is today.

Carrots for Clients

Customers want to know you care.

⌒⌒

We've all been stuck in an airplane on the tarmac. It's aggravating and sometimes infuriating—especially when you have no idea what's going on.

However, when the captain's voice finally booms confidently through the intercom apprising you of the situation, it is comforting. He may be announcing that you're third in line for takeoff or delivering the bad news that another storm is moving in and you're not going anywhere for a while. Either way, we'd rather know what's going on than be kept in the dark.

Give your clients a carrot. Respect them enough to communicate with them whether news is good or bad. The fact that you're talking and working to find solutions speaks volumes about you and your company.

CARROT ACTION: Look out for your clients. Respect them by keeping them in the loop, so they know you're taking care of them. You'll be creating trust and nurturing a great working relationship.

When laughter goes viral

Time out for fun.
—Devo

In the course of a long day behind a computer, you inevitably encounter links to disparate humorous postings on the Internet. Typically these include the latest viral TV commercial, blooper, or Web comedy short. Your friends or family members "stumble across" (Google search) these clips and they simply *must* pass them on.

Rather than furrow your brows and give the evil eye to those near you who may be gathered around a monitor cackling with laughter at the latest must-see video, suggest that a certain time of day be scheduled for a daily team viewing. Then you can gather for five minutes and share a laugh together, stay current on what's making the rounds, and take a much needed and deserved break from your desk chair.

CARROT ACTION: Take the initiative to formalize the get-together. Think it through and select an appropriate time of day. Write up a humorous email invite and include a link to a short, hilarious clip to illustrate the point.

The Welcome Party

Cheer for the one who answers the challenge.

". . . And so the brave knight returned in triumph to the empty streets of his village. He slopped his pigs and went to bed. No one seemed to care that the village was no longer terrorized by the terrible dragon. So the knight put away his sword and lived a quiet, anonymous life, dying gently in his sleep one winter day."

This is not the kind of ending you, or the knight, would have anticipated, and it's certainly not a happy one. Unfortunately, though, it's *exactly* the ending you get in a company that lacks recognition programs.

Within these companies, talented and energetic employees are repeatedly overlooked, until, disappointed by the lack of reaction to their heroic efforts, they put away their swords and wait out their careers in a half sleep or move on to more promising territory.

It doesn't have to be that way. The solution lies in employee recognition—the modern hero's welcome.

CARROT ACTION: Decide today to head the welcome party. Remember to make sure the honors at this party are specific to the hero's accomplishments—and, of course, timely.

Kind Words

Always forgive your enemies—
nothing annoys them so much.
—Oscar Wilde

It's been said that in business that nice guys finish last. And, let's face it, sometimes it's much more difficult to say a kind word than it is to thrust verbal daggers through the hearts of the people you disagree with.

Cutthroat, competitive, and crushing business practices can win in the short term—but they are rarely successful over the long haul.

True leaders are those who communicate kindness, forgiveness, and understanding. They recognize the people who helped them climb the ladder of success rather than smashing others out of their way. They lead because people want to follow—not because those people fear not following them.

CARROT ACTION: Practice forgiveness today. Communicate that forgiveness and move on. Even your enemies will realize that you are leading a positive way forward.

Boomerang

What goes out almost always comes back—eventually.

⌒⌒

The other day, one of us found a note slipped under the door of his office. It was from a person we had not seen in almost a year. When we opened it, we were surprised to find a thank-you note—for things we had done a long time ago. So long ago, in fact, that we had all but forgotten them.

The timing was perfect. It had been a rough day—actually, a rough week—and reading those kinds words made us realize that although we may not see the results of our efforts right away, nothing is done in vain.

CARROT ACTION: Try to initiate the Boomerang Effect. The recognition you give away always finds its way back to you.

Are you interesting?

*The way to gain a good reputation
is to endeavor to be what you desire to be.*
—Socrates

Think about the people you know who are interesting—not necessarily likeable, enjoyable, or popular, but interesting.

Interesting people are interested. Interesting people are passionate about something. They have purpose. And, even if we don't agree with, understand, or even like the aspects of their lives they feel are of utmost importance, such people are undeniably interesting.

Your accountant has wallpapered her entire office with photos of her cat. Your sister-in-law thinks a certain political party is directly aligned with the devil. Your cousin Jimmy is convinced he's created the next great breakfast cereal.

These people are interesting simply because they're interested in something. Show off your interests and promote the sense that it's okay to be human.

CARROT ACTION: If you want to be considered "good" in your role, get interested in your audience. Good team members are interested in their co-workers. Good husbands are interested in their wives. Good parents are interested in their children. And, good employees are interested in their work. Write down the things that interest you.

Innovation

*In the most innovative companies there is
a significantly higher volume of thank-yous
than in companies of low innovation.*
—Rosabeth Moss Kanter

If you and your co-workers have been using the same routine for a few too many years, it may be time to reinvent yourselves. And that means it's time for a little brainstorming.

In order to reinvent, reenergize, and reinvigorate the creative geniuses among you, start appreciating the small, wacky, and out-of-the-box ideas that people come up with. Praise the great ideas *and* the stupid ideas. Keep praising each other, and as you do, you'll find that the ideas will continue to grow more innovative. When we know that someone is actually paying attention to, and praising, the suggestions we give, we're more likely to continue to offer our creative thoughts and ideas.

CARROT ACTION: Today, pay attention and be open to new ideas for old problems. Try tackling a familiar daily routine in a new and different way and see what happens.

Assume Some Blame

Perpetuating mediocrity is an inherently depressing process and drains much more energy out of the pool than it puts back in.
—Jim Collins

In a mediocre work environment a lot of blame is thrown around. A deal goes south, someone is to blame. A customer is disappointed, and fingers start pointing. Co-workers are thrown under the bus left and right, with a resulting decrease in trust and productivity.

When team members spend their time looking for others to blame, everyone is distracted. The team starts to splinter as team members take sides. Rather than perpetuate these negative cycles, the next time a co-worker throws you under the bus, readily accept your share of the blame, learn from it, and move on. Don't spend your time or energy on arguing these trivial matters.

CARROT ACTION: The next time you consider throwing a co-worker under the bus, stop. Don't do it. Accept your responsibility in the situation and move on.

Be a Good Sport

Could be worse. Could be raining.

It's inevitable that the spinning bottle of recognition will ultimately point in your direction. Yes, you will be "caught" doing something praiseworthy: pitching in to bail someone else out, coming up with a hot new product, handling a customer crisis, or even just hitting the ten-year mark of employment with your sanity.

Whatever your accomplishment, your boss will wish to celebrate you in front of your co-workers not only to give you your just desserts, but also to motivate others to similar levels of achievement.

Our need to be recognized, however, is typically buried, sometimes even fooling us; consciously we would deny ourselves of any "nonsensical pomp," but on a subconscious level the need exists.

Let your inner self win the battle. If your boss wishes to talk you up to your workmates, let him. Even if you'd rather deflect the praise or "aw shucks" your way out of it, allow others to do their jobs in celebrating you.

CARROT ACTION: If anyone pays you any compliment at all today smile and say, "Well, thank you, that's very kind of you!" and nothing else.

Celebrate Birthdays

Let them eat cake.

Your company may not recognize birthdays, but that doesn't mean you can't. Taking ten minutes at some point to pull your co-workers together to sing "Happy Birthday" and honor an associate on his or her special day is a surefire way to show a little love.

You should also take it upon yourself to say a few words of praise about the person of honor. Don't be afraid to tie his birthday to how grateful you are that he works with you and for all the great things he brings to the workplace each day.

CARROT ACTION: Volunteer to be the department's first birthday coordinator. Keep track of everyone's b-day. Be the one to start planning and make it happen.

Accountable to What?

*Happiness is the state of consciousness
which proceeds from achievement of one's values.*
—Ayn Rand

Most people will say that finding a "job" that satisfies their innermost passion is their dream. While many people cruise Internet job boards while they're on the clock, there are also those who, no matter how choppy the waves at the office, work diligently while waiting for the storm to blow past. Ask these people if they love their job and they'll probably respond with something like, "it's okay." But ask them why they don't search calmer waters, and they'll probably say something like, "I believe in what we do here."

People seek purpose, and they identify with others who share their purpose and with companies that have clear missions. Although procedures, processes, and deadlines often drive people's actions, they are not what make people accountable for the long run. We are accountable when we believe in a cause and have a sense of ownership in the outcome.

CARROT ACTION: Research shows that "pride in the corporate symbol" truly drives employee engagement. Review your company's mission statement to remind yourself why you're there. Or, take note of what you feel the next time you see your company logo. Are you proud to be a part of its purpose?

Tweet, Tweet

Find the best way to communicate.

⌒

Being able to communicate with your team members is one
key to a successful career. The better the communication the
better the results.

But people understand concepts in different ways, and
different media are suitable for different people. Great business people understand that some of their associates need
face time, others want to talk via phone, others text, while
some prefer email. Note how to reach each of your team in
a way that they best understand and respond to. If it means
you need to Facebook or Twitter, then get online.

CARROT ACTION: Ask each team member the best way to reach
him or her. Do the needs vary by age, job title, etc.? Seek to
tailor your missives to ensure that they will properly hit the
mark every time.

It's the Chilies

Spice up your communication to get a response.

Food Product Design magazine claims salsa is now the number one condiment in the United States. Somehow it surpassed ketchup as the favorite.

Apparently salsa is being more widely used—spicing up more items today—than its competitors. It's most likely due to the fact that spice creates an immediate response.

Does salsa work with, or improve, everything? Well, very few things do. In work and life, there isn't always a clear-cut, one-stop solution to everything. However, there is one thing that can make any communication improve: spice it up.

The more interesting your communication, the more people will pay attention. Humor, stories, statistics, and human interest make messages more accessible and memorable.

CARROT ACTION: Practice your communication with someone you trust. Ask for feedback—the raw truth. Then get ready to set your work world ablaze with communication that creates an immediate response.

Think. Grow. Own.

Effort only fully releases its reward
after a person refuses to quit.
—Napoleon Hill

Accountability isn't defined by success, but by perseverance to achieve a planned-for outcome. Most successful entrepreneurs have, on more than one occasion, experienced great failure. Learning from the mistakes improved their next endeavor and eventually led them to great breakthroughs.

Accountability means just that—you own the process, you own the outcome, and you own the responsibility of success or failure. There is value in either outcome.

CARROT ACTION: Document your failures—small and large—in a journal. Consider them part of the process to improvement.

The Credo

Point others in the right direction.

Does your organization have a formal credo, a vision or values statement? Do all your employees know what that statement is and what it means to your department? If they don't, talk about the statement in your next recognition celebration.

For example, "I wanted to gather to recognize Julie today. Our company credo says we believe in teamwork, and nobody epitomizes that better than Julie. Just last month, I was complaining about not being able to get the information we needed from accounting. So Julie set up weekly meetings with our contact over there. I know I speak for all of us when I say things are vastly improved now, due to Julie's teamwork."

CARROT ACTION: Recognition ceremonies are communication opportunities. They are the perfect time to reinforce what is most important to you and your organization.

Precise and Concise Are Nice

*If I am to speak ten minutes, I need a week
for preparation; if fifteen minutes, three days;
if half an hour, two days; if an hour, I am ready now.*
—Woodrow Wilson

What if every word you spoke created the exact outcome you intended? What if:

> "The garbage is full," actually got the trash taken out.
> "I'm between jobs," got you the career of your dreams.
> "I really shouldn't eat this," actually stopped you from eating it.

Communication is tricky because it matters more what the listener hears than what the speaker says. And often it's the ambiguous sayings that miss the goal of effective communication. Be clear, repeat, and then do it again.

CARROT ACTION: Choose three simple instances in your life where you wish people would respond more positively to your communication. Write down your typical word choices in one column. Then rewrite the message using more interesting wording, stories, or examples. Then give it a try. You'll be amazed at how simple tweaks to your vocabulary can create dramatic results.

Melody

Each of us is the lead singer of our song.

Even though your voice might not be intended for the concert stage, you're still the maestro of your own melody. You sing your own song, walk to the beat of your own drum, and so forth . . . at least until it's time to join the band.

As individuals, it's important to have unique identities and dreams. But it's also important to understand that it's often the "band" that helps us find our own stage.

Where do you draw the line between your dreams and the band's dreams?

- Dependency: Don't go there, it means you can't operate without them.
- Independence: Don't go there either. It means you'll succeed, but you'll be lonesome and you'll miss out on the input and energy of others.
- Interdependence: This is where you want to be. Everyone has their own identities but you all leverage your talents to create beautiful music.

CARROT ACTION: Pretend you're forming a rock band with your team. Who would be vocals? Who would play bass guitar? What attitude does each player bring to the stage? And, at what part of the song does each player get to crank out a solo?

Crisis? What Crisis?

*It feels like a time to panic . . .
but your boss might not agree.*

⌒

You and your co-workers have been working on a project for weeks now and it's just about done. It's coming down to the wire, but you and the team are going to make the deadline and the entire project will be a huge success.

But suddenly there's a problem. The client calls and wants just a few "little" changes made; oh, and he still needs the project completed on time. This little newsflash creates pandemonium among the team.

So, you'd better rush into your boss's office and blurt out the entire story, then seek advice. Right? In most cases, that's the wrong thing to do.

Your boss is dealing with her own crises. This situation may be a challenge for you, but it isn't necessarily for her. So take control. As a team, you can most often solve the issue yourselves. Put your heads together and make it happen.

CARROT ACTION: Try not to turn to your boss with every crisis. Solve most problems yourself and your boss will appreciate your self-sufficiency and admire your leadership.

Build

Better the lives of others.

For years, psychologists have known the rule of 5 to 1. Praise should outweigh criticism by five to one in a positive relationship—parent/child, husband/wife, coach/player, and boss/employee.

And don't forget, praise should be public, coaching should be private.

CARROT ACTION: Take note today of how many positive comments you make to co-workers versus "coaching" comments.

Repetition. Repetition. Repetition.

If real estate is about location, goals are about practice.

In the movie *The Karate Kid*, wimpy nerd Daniel La Russo waxes cars, paints fences, and sands decks—all with instructions that include precise arm movements. Of course, Daniel believes he is just doing chores, until his *sensei*, Mr. Miyagi shows him that he has been, in fact, practicing blocking techniques—and the repetition is a means of teaching.

Goal setting in the workplace must include time for repetition, practicing your art, so by the time you reach your goal, you've mastered each maneuver. If your goal is to give better presentations, practice in front of the mirror. If you want to close more sales, practice making the pitch. Discipline yourself to become a master.

CARROT ACTION: Name three things you're doing today to practice the skills that will help you reach your goals. Are you honing your craft, increasing your speed, or working on finding a perfect balance between your current responsibilities and your goal timeline? Name three things every day. They may change as you make progress.

Squeeze It In.

Make an appointment with yourself.

Make regular recognition a habit by scheduling dates on your calendar. Months ahead plans days that you'll recognize someone—anticipating projects due, milestones reached, goals achieved. This week, write in your day planner that you will publicly recognize someone on your team this week.

CARROT ACTION: You can move it to another day, but this act has to be completed by Friday.

Carrots for Life

Rural Carrots.

⌒⌒

We've personally had opportunities recently to work at summer camps for the Boy Scouts and other youth groups where our job was to motivate and lead a group of kids to act as kitchen crew, cleanup, or volunteer counselors.

In each case we were thrilled to be able to use the power of *frequent, specific,* and *timely* Carrots. It's amazing how quickly these adolescents (who are often, ahem, a little lazy) began to rise early and work hard for the smallest token of appreciation: a stuffed, plush Carrot (Garrett, our iconic mascot—see our blogs if you'd like to get a look).

Additionally, beyond the tangible tokens of thanks, we also offered small verbal Carrots: specific, public praise and pats on the back that pointed out the little things they did well to make the camps run smoothly.

The better you get at this kind of cheap, informal recognition at work, the more you can use it in your outside associations.

CARROT ACTION: Ask yourself in what other ways you can apply Carrot Principles in your personal life.

Change Your Tune.
Change Your Brand.

*When you are in a room and your job is to write jokes
ten hours a day, your mind starts going to strange places.*
—Seth MacFarlane

Communication can be shared between two people. It can
be internal dialogue. It can be broadcast to masses. The way
you choose to communicate will affect the way you and
your team operate.

Brand management companies communicate the essence
of organizations—and sometimes the communication of
that essence changes that essence.

If you want to move your group, yourself, or your entire
organization in a new direction, start by communicating the
direction you're headed today, and compare that to where
you'd like to be headed. Your new direction may seem strange
to many, but most great ideas seem a little odd at first.

CARROT ACTION: Want to really have some fun? Communicate your personal brand by telling your story through the
eyes of your favorite fictional character. Just changing your
tune, your voice, and your perspective will open your eyes to
unimaginable opportunities.

In Their Shoes

Walk a mile.

When facing stretched budgets for recognition or appreciation, look for low-cost/no-cost Carrots. Quite often, they can be the most effective.

For example, everyone has a task or duty they hate. Maybe it's a regular inventory report, putting together an expense sheet, collecting the carts out in the parking lot, or handling a heated customer with a warranty claim.

If you sincerely wish to show gratitude to a co-worker for what she does, do her least favorite task for her. Give her a rest. It shows that you understand what might really be the most valuable reward for her labor, creativity, and results: a little break from it all.

It doesn't cost a cent, but the returns are priceless.

CARROT ACTION: Ask yourself if there's someone on the team that does a tough job you might help with as a one-time reward for him or her. Is there an opportunity for you to apply this type of Carrot? If so, do it.

Recognition Grab Bag

You never know what you're gonna get. Except smiles.

Spend a few bucks at the Dollar Store and have an ever-ready supply of recognition at your fingertips. A bag of plastic army men for those who "soldiered on" with that last proposal, a brightly colored pinwheel for the person who is the "wind in the sails" of the team . . . you get the idea.

Campy? Sure. Embrace the campiness. Revel in it. Love the campy. People will catch on. These little tidbits become symbols of what your co-workers have done. These are day-to-day reminders that someone cares about what they do.

CARROT ACTION: Remember the special treat box at the dentist? Same idea, but less pain.

The Gamblers

Take a risk on accountability

The stakes:

1. The salesperson with the most prospecting calls at the end of the day gets tomorrow afternoon off.
2. If the company reaches its year-end safety goal, the CEO will buy lunch one day next week.
3. If the entire team exceeds its goals by 15 percent, the boss will shave half of his beard and mustache, the left half.

Often times, bets are made to increase competitiveness and performance in the workplace—positive consequences for success, and negative for failure. The tactic is alive and well in workplaces all over the world. However, very few individuals hold themselves accountable to accountability. Make sure your team takes calculated risks now and then, and make sure you follow up on the rewards to enhance your trustworthiness.

CARROT ACTION: Take a risk. Establish positive and negative consequences. Set your goal, set wacky stakes, and see what kind of shenanigans you can get yourself into.

A Hall of Fame File

For the do-it-yourselfers.

We each have a file at the office that isn't opened very often, but proves invaluable every time we do. We call it the Hall of Fame File.

It's filled with positive performance appraisals, thank-you cards, awards, personal notes from family and friends—anything that validates us as people and professionals. Of course, there's always room for more.

CARROT ACTION: Start your file today. On days when you really need a little emotional pick-me-up or self-esteem booster, but none seems to be forthcoming from those around you, open the file and, voilà! instant recognition.

Champion Your Goal

Pain is temporary. Quitting lasts forever.
—Lance Armstrong

Eric Jones was an accountant with a passion for motocross. He was a talented rider who spent his weekends at the local track—upstaging the other locals who didn't take the sport so seriously. Eric's times on the track were impressive, even competitive with nationally ranked riders. In fact, his skills might even be good enough to make him a professional rider.

One weekend, Eric's friend persuaded him to enter an actual competition. They packed up the trailer. They loaded the bikes. And they set off on a four-hour road-trip where Eric might make his dream a reality.

Today, Eric is still an accountant. He never entered that race, fearing that his dream would be crushed, he decided at the last minute not to suit up. Dream unfulfilled, Eric still wonders "what if?"

CARROT ACTION: Goal setting must be approached without fear of failure. Remember, failure is curable. Become your own champion and cheering section today—not necessarily to win, but just to participate in working toward your goal.

Family Time

Blending home and office.

Invite the family of a recognized person to attend a recognition event in his honor. Performance awards, service awards, sales awards, and other forms of recognition are wonderful opportunities to bring family members into work.

And remember, a retirement celebration should *never* be held without the honoree's family in attendance.

CARROT ACTION: Next time you invite a family to attend, ask those family members to add a few words of their own.

Voicemail

Put your money where your mouth is.

There's a difference between a voicemail and a *voicemail*. Turn off Styxx (you know who you are) for three minutes on your drive to or from work to leave a memorable, meaningful *voicemail* or two. Instead of asking for something to get done or if something got done, compliment someone, say thanks, or remind someone of the difference he or she makes in your work life, or in that of the team, or the organization.

It's amazing the return you'll see on very little effort.

CARROT ACTION: Plan what you are going to say before you make the call. Then charge your Bluetooth *before* you get in the car.

In All the Wrong Places

*The real tragedy of life is not that each of us
doesn't have enough strengths, it's that we fail
to use the ones we have.*
—Marcus Buckingham and Donald Clifton

A young woman was raised by strong parents who instilled in her a great work ethic. Early on in her education, this young girl's future career was decided by helpful parents and teachers—she should be a pharmacist. The need for pharmacists was great, and the job would give her financial stability.

When she became a pharmacist, stability was achieved, but did this young girl achieve her goals?

"My job is okay," the now-respected pharmacist explained. "But, I always liked writing, and being creative. There's not much room for those types of activities as a pharmacist."

Goal setting is an important element of your success. However, if you allow others to control or interfere with your goals, they aren't truly *your* goals.

CARROT ACTION: Forget your current job situation. Choose one goal you'd like to pursue that doesn't complement your current job, schedule, or responsibilities. Create an action plan to achieve that goal within the next ten years. You'll find that simply writing down your plan presents new ideas for reaching your goal much sooner than you might have thought.

Silent Majority

A rooster crows only when it sees the light.
Put him in the dark and he'll never crow.
I have seen the light and I'm crowing.
—Muhammad Ali

Every job description should include instructions to "share ideas for improvement, state your opinion, and take a stand if you believe it's in the best interest of the organization."

Too often employees are asked to perform a function, and assumptions are made that they will speak up if they see a better way. But research shows that employees don't feel they have the right to share ideas, that their ideas aren't valued, or that sharing their ideas is actually not allowed.

What happens when any of the above is true? Employees talk about their frustrations among their teammates. Good ideas get squashed by mistrust. And productivity, innovation, and the organization's potential suffer—all due to a lack of communication.

CARROT ACTION: It takes at least two parties to share, and sharing should be equal. Today, whether you're an employee, manager, director, or even a member of another type of group (family, community, neighborhood, etc.) (1) make a point to share, and (2) make a point to ask for others' opinions. That means that you take a turn, and you request that others take a turn.

Show and Tell

Don't just say it, show it.

⌒

When it comes to recognition in the work environment, it's essential to "show" while you "tell."

If you want your people engaged in a joint cause, make your recognition efforts strategic. This is why public recognition is important, because it broadcasts your company's core values and business strategy. It shows your employees the kind of behavior you're looking for.

For instance, it's one thing to say "teamwork" is a core value. It's another thing to catch an employee practicing "teamwork" and then publicly laud her for it. The presentation *shows* exactly what teamwork looks like in your organization. You're basically saying, "This is what it means when we talk about this otherwise abstract value. This is the kind of behavior we want repeated."

How will employees know what is valued at your company if they don't have a realistic example of it?

CARROT ACTION: When you see a co-worker really demonstrating the core values and executing the business strategy, let him know that you noticed and were impressed. Gather everyone around and praise your peer for epitomizing what is important at your company.

Seeds of Engagement

Develop an award to grow on.

One particularly green company we've worked with plants a tree in an outstanding employee's name. This not only helps the environment, but is a lasting reminder of the company's appreciation for this person's great work.

CARROT ACTION: To make a real statement, go a little farther. Start a Grove of Champions by planting the tree on the company lawn, with a small (but permanent) name marker, then adding to the grove over time. Can't go that far? How about presenting a plant to green up the office?

Peer Pressure

Walk and talk like T-Birds

Danny Zuko fell in love one summer. The girl was beautiful, smart, sweet, and not at all his type. He was a T-Bird—fast cars, fast motorcycles, and leather jackets. Somehow they made it work.

The popularity of the movie and the play, *Grease*, is due to the fact that it struck a nerve, revealing the struggles of youth, love, and reputation maintenance.

All of us belong to subcultures, peer groups, and teams. Those groups have expectations of us as leaders, innovators, executors, managers, and organizers.

Are we accountable to the expectations of our subcultures?

The answer to that question can be argued for eternity. But the truth of the matter is actually quite simple. We are accountable not only to those groups we belong to, but more importantly to what we know is right. Expand your horizons. It's your choice, Danny boy!

CARROT ACTION: Take inventory of your accountability. Think of it like a closet. You don't have to keep everything; only keep the things that move you forward through the next season. Is it time to rethink an organizational membership, a project that doesn't add value, a routine that distracts from your goal? With less clutter, you'll be much more effective.

Favorites

The resource next door.

Ask your neighbors and friends to tell you about their favorite recognition moments, even if they occurred years ago in school. Understanding how people felt when they were recognized, especially if they still remember presentations that happened long ago, can only help you become a more successful businessperson. Successful people make others feel appreciated, drawing others to them.

CARROT ACTION: By Friday, ask two neighbors to share their fond memories.

Gratitude Is Riches

Stop the complaining.

It's easy to find stuff to complain about at work—your co-workers, the computer that runs too slow, tough assignments, fluorescent lighting, cafeteria food that even farm animals would refuse. We go on and on, don't we? And when we hear a co-worker complaining, it's easy to jump on the bandwagon and include our two cents. Before long the complaining is creating animosity with us and management, and our work environment has become toxic.

We've all done our share of complaining around the office. The time to stop is now; and *you* have to be the one to stop it.

When a co-worker starts complaining, change the subject and find something to praise. You are going to have to be the example and initiate change. As you start to focus on the positive things, other co-workers will follow suit. It may take a while, but don't give up. It's worth it to create a more copacetic, engaging work environment for all.

CARROT ACTION: Today, find something to praise about work instead of criticize. Praise a co-worker, praise your boss, heck, you could even find something to praise about the lunchroom fare. Gratitude is riches; complaint is poverty.

Dream Team

We must all hang together, or assuredly,
we shall all hang separately.
—Benjamin Franklin

Charles Batcheldor was a machinist. John Kruesi was a clockmaker. Ludwig Boehm was a glassblower. Francis Upton was a mathematician. Together, they shared a vision with an inventor: Thomas Edison. Together they created the light bulb.

Stories of great teams inspire us all to find those puzzle-piece people in our own lives that inspire us to reach farther, deeper, and give our best and to contribute to the making of a stellar product. It is when these people share their strengths and talents that goals are extended—reaching sometimes beyond our imagination. And, as in Edison's case, they can change the world as we know it.

A single goal is powerful. A combined goal changes the parameters of what can be accomplished.

CARROT ACTION: Goal share. Set aside some time to connect with your team. Discover new ways to leverage strengths, relationships, and networks.

Thrift Store Magic

Easy. Fun. CHEAP. Did we mention CHEAP?

Stop by the Goodwill or the Salvation Army and pick up something that'll pick up your people. Whether it's literally a trophy (that six foot bowling monster trophy is sure to make an impression) or any another simple symbol of your appreciation, you might be surprised how your co-workers will "adopt" the thing. One man's trash becomes another's motivational treasure. Seriously, the velvet pirate-ship painting? Recognition GOLD. There's nothing wrong with an award or two in your culture that add humor and fun.

These trinkets will become legendary coveted talismans of teamwork, sacrifice, and achievement. People will pass them around with reverence and care. The item may be silly, but the results won't be.

CARROT ACTION: Swing by the local thrift store on your way home. Ignore that sweet leather coat with the fringe and keep your co-workers in mind.

Details, Details, Details

Is this title too vague to communicate anything valuable?

There are shortcuts in the English language—acronyms, abbreviations, pronouns, proverbs, and even prepositions. But problems can occur when we use shortcuts. Although brevity doesn't necessarily mean ambiguity, all too often shortcuts in communication can lead to detours in execution.

For example, "Get it done" means what? We assume that when we say those words, people understand it's time to really hit our goals. But, let's analyze this brief statement.

1. What does "Get" mean? Depending on the task, it could mean process, obtain, write, integrate, summarize, outline, hone, adjust, etc.
2. What does "it" mean? It could mean project, paper, report, presentation, etc.
3. What does "done" mean? It could mean repaired, processed, analyzed, secured, marketed . . . you get the idea.

Today, many of us move so fast that we miss the details and spread confusion. Communicate briefly. Communicate concisely. But never forget to communicate in detail.

CARROT ACTION: Record yourself in a typical conversation. Transcribe three sentences to see where you take shortcuts in communication that may be hurting clarity. Adjust your language for precision and test your revised statements on a co-worker.

Blush and Take It

How to accept responsibility for being a rock star.

⌒

The late Jim Morrison began his music career by singing with his back to the audience. And, although fans swooned to see the face of the young "Mr. Mojo Risin'" they had to wait until he could turn and accept their applause.

Accepting accountability for our actions—positive or negative—is a valued trait. And, although sometimes it's embarrassing to accept praise for a job well done, or an effort well executed, it's important to allow others to recognize us.

Turn around, Jim, and face the audience. Look up, Sue. Your boss is smiling at your performance. And Craig, accept that your wife appreciates the fact that you do know how to pick up your socks. Learn to accept the consequences of your good behaviors without embarrassment.

CARROT ACTION: Become your own fan today. Recognize the accomplishments you've achieved that have made you proud this month. Give yourself a pat on the back and own your success. This will help you to accept praise when it comes from others.

Sincerity

*One of the most effective ways to motivate known
to man is one of the most simple: a compliment.*
—Adrian Gostick and Chester Elton

The truth, the whole truth, and nothing but the truth. That's the golden rule for giving compliments. (And, as it happens, it works well in the courtroom, too.)

You should never feel the need to embellish a co-worker's accomplishment nor to exaggerate her impact. When giving a compliment, simply say what you mean and mean what you say. If you don't, it will show and your good intentions will be wasted.

Instead of "you do great work," try, "Thanks for finding that defect in the component yesterday. We were able to live our core value of 'no defects.' Thanks so much." A big difference.

CARROT ACTION: Sincerity comes most naturally when complimenting behaviors that truly advance team goals. Be on the lookout for those types of activities. When you've found one, go ahead and tell the employee the truth: that his actions make the company a success, and that you're truly grateful.

No Hot Air

Set their spirits soaring.

Where it might be inappropriate to send flowers to an employee, it's hardly ever inappropriate to send balloons. Send a balloon bouquet to a great employee to recognize her for above-and-beyond achievement.

CARROT ACTION: If you're feeling particularly generous, take a hit of helium before you express your gratitude verbally. Make everyone laugh, grab their attention, and then make your point. Everyone will be listening.

Necessary Tools

Goal setting is a pathway for activity.

Ask any do-it-yourself handyman or woman what the two most valuable home repair products are on the market. Inevitably you'll hear these two answers: (1) duct tape, and (2) WD-40.

Duct tape makes things stick. WD-40 gets things unstuck.

Visualize your goal setting as a home improvement project. Set your goals with duct tape (make them stick). Now visualize your hurdles and responsibilities as another project. Lube those up with WD-40 (remove them from your path).

CARROT ACTION: Make a goal-setting and achievement tool chest. This will require a calendar, a detailed explanation of your goal, and an I-owe-you letter written to yourself promising a reward. Use these tools daily to track progress and keep your eye on the prize.

Your Map

*Goals are road maps that show us
what is possible in life.*

Dr. Dwight Lundell, a retired heart surgeon, was crossing items off his "bucket list" before his sixty-fifth birthday. One of those items was to complete a full length triathlon, a feat that he hadn't even considered twenty years earlier. He trained. He groaned. He woke up daily fearing that he may have missed his opportunity in life to have the physical stamina to achieve his goal—finishing a competition that is typically reserved for younger athletes.

Race day arrived. Dr. Lundell completed the 2.4 mile swim. He completed his 112 mile bike ride. He completed the 26.2 mile run. And then he died. Just kidding; he actually finished first in his age group, resulting in another item for his bucket list: a qualifying spot at the IronMan World Championship in Kona, Hawaii.

And initially all he had wanted to do was finish. Look what you can accomplish when you set your sights on a goal, no matter how impossible the journey might seem at the outset.

CARROT ACTION: Press your luck today. Set a daily goal that seems impossible to accomplish. Keep that goal until you succeed. You'll be surprised at what awaits you on the horizon.

Black Hole

What doesn't get said?

Every one of us has a friend, a relative, or a co-worker whose long pauses between words or thoughts make us uncomfortable.

We are not talking about someone with a speech impediment, but just a slow talker. A real thinker. Got your "black hole" conversationalist in mind?

In this stress-filled world, gaping holes in conversation can drive us batty. Why?

Communication isn't only about what we say. It's also about all the stuff we don't say. We start to wonder about those holes in conversation. What do they mean?

It's our job to fill in gaps for conversational counterparts. That doesn't mean constant chatter. It simply means that with or without words, we're consistently saying something positive to our audience.

CARROT ACTION: Who is the quietest person on your team, the person you know the least about. Have an uninterrupted conversation with *her*. Ask open-ended questions like: How are you? How could I help you? What's going on around here? You'll be shocked at what you learn about that person.

A Secret Recipe

Cook up some results.

The next time you have an unusually challenging group goal, up the ante a little. Announce that you will personally cook the team breakfast—or barbeque them lunch, whatever is your specialty—when the goal is attained. If you can, flip the pancakes in the office instead of bringing them in.

Recognition is the best communication vehicle we have. And when you take the time to prepare a meal for your team, you communicate that they matter and you are willing to sacrifice in return for the hard work they give.

CARROT ACTION: The key here is that you actually do the cooking. Don't hand it off to someone else.

Sweatin' to the Oldies?

Coaches who can outline plays on a blackboard
are a dime a dozen. The ones who win
get inside their player and motivate.
—Vince Lombardi

One of the largest industries in America today is the diet industry. Every couple of years a new theory is released— a new meal plan, a new sport, and a new contraption that promises something like "six-pack abs without any effort."

Of course, science continually reveals more interesting facts about the human body, and this information influences the way we eat, exercise, and live. Yet if you look at the influencers in this field—the people who have truly shaped (pardon the pun) a nation—a curly-haired, overtly rambunctious, nonscientific little man still remains one of the diet industry's powerhouses of change.

Richard Simmons motivated you to lose weight, but not by being a too-perfect guru. He was simply enthusiastic and asked you to join in. He cranked up the oldies. He told you to break a sweat, but he did it by having fun. That's what great motivators do. They make us work hard, and yet we feel like we are having fun.

CARROT ACTION: Define your motivation strategy. How will you motivate yourself? How will you motivate your team? Like Simmons, how can you throw some fun into the mix?

Make Up Your Mind

If it gets any better, it wouldn't be fair.
—Dalton Elton (Chester's father)

Happiness isn't something that you can be given. It isn't something that arrives one day, like a package, when the conditions are just right. It's a choice. It's a decision. His Holiness the Dalai Lama reminds us, "Happiness mainly comes from our own attitude, rather than from external factors. If your own mental attitude is correct, even if you remain in a hostile atmosphere, you feel happy."

So it's ironic that so many of us who are paid to make decisions every day in business can't seem to make up our minds to simply be positive. Stop feeling sorry for yourself, appreciate the good things in your life and at work, and make a conscious decision to improve the situation for the better.

CARROT ACTION: Today, make it a goal to remain unruffled no matter what happens around you. When people ask you, "How's it going?" answer, "If it gets any better, it wouldn't be fair!" As you adopt a cheerful, positive attitude, you will feel happier in your job. And so will those around you.

Theme Week

Put some spice in their coffee (not literally!).

⌐⌐

Make an otherwise boring workweek a little more exciting by giving co-workers something to look forward to. Theme weeks, as silly or as appropriate as *you* make them, can be that extra something that gets people excited to come to work.

A new and exotic coffee flavor (and soda for the non-java crowd) week. A different movie theme M–F. Historical character week. Book character week. Wear a different color each day. Subtle metaphor week. Dress up, decorate, do whatever you feel works to make your environment more stimulating. One workplace we visited has dress up days monthly with parades around the office and prizes for the best costumes. It may not add much to the bottom line, but people are lining up to work there and morale and creativity are sky high.

Again, make it as silly or serious or appropriate as you and your team can handle. Give it a shot.

CARROT ACTION: The more energy and creativity you invest, the more likely people are to buy in.

Universal Language

*One nice thing eez, the game of love eez never
called on account of darkness.*
—Pepe Le Pew

Trying times are among us all—economic hurdles, stress, and
anxiety about the future can be overwhelming. Understand
that your co-workers and your loved ones are stressed too,
and they need appreciation more than you might realize.

Remember that some forms of communication are effective regardless of the dark times and the challenges. One
form of communication is the language of love, and the
other is the language of gratitude.

Saying "I love you" never loses its impact. And, neither
does saying thanks. Practice them both vigorously for the
best results.

CARROT ACTION: Can we say it enough? Recognition must be
communicated. Say "thank you" as much as possible. Be specific to what you're showing gratitude. And, as a word to the
wise, be specific to the people that you tell, "I love you."

!

Excitement? Anger? Joy?

⌐⌐

The exclamation point is overused. It's vague, it's tired, and it needs a break.

Krista, a mortgage broker in Minneapolis, was returning to the office after maternity leave. This company email was sent to employees on her floor:

"Krista is back from maternity leave so make her feel welcome! There will be a gathering in the break room at noon to congratulate her on her baby boy! Enjoy sandwiches and treats—on the company! We will see you there!"

Okay, so we know the intention was to show excitement for Krista. And in this case a few exclamation points were actually necessary because the words are rather cold and insincere. But it would have been better for the email's author to choose his words wisely in order to limit the use of exclamation points. Here's a good example of a better way to write the same message:

"Krista, we're all thrilled and overjoyed to welcome you back. You were greatly missed, and we look forward to meeting baby Kyle. From the pictures, he looks adorable. Hey, let's celebrate—sandwiches for everybody in the break room at noon!"

CARROT ACTION: Avoid overuse of exclamation points in writing, but do add them to your sentences when you speak. Get excited about your life, your job, your friends, and your future.

The Challenge of Being New

Remember your first day on the job?

Think back to your first day at work. Not only did you have new procedures and product details to master, but you also had new co-workers. And no matter if you are starting as a senior executive or a cashier, new co-workers are frightening. Will they like you? Will they feel you are competent? Will they accept you as part of the team? Heck, will they invite you to lunch?

Openly welcome new employees. Offer to help them out in any way—and then make sure to do so. Offer to answer any questions they might have—and then listen and answer patiently. Invite their "outside perspective" on a project. Create a mini-celebration of doughnuts and juice to welcome them to the team. The sense of belonging that your new co-worker will feel will be priceless. The new guy will instantly feel like he's part of the team, which will help him get up to speed that much quicker.

CARROT ACTION: Invite a newer employee to lunch today. Get to know the new person. Don't you wish someone had taken you under his wing on *your* first day?

The Right Direction

Have confidence that if you have done a little thing well,
you can do a bigger thing well too.
—David Storey

What if sports fans reserved their applause only for the winning team at the end of the game? Or if no one yelled encouragement during the match? No giant foam No. 1 hands waving in the air. No enormous painted bellies. It would take away a lot of the fun and excitement and much of the players' motivation.

The same goes for the office. Don't hold back recognition until a project's completion. Celebrate the little landmarks along the way.

CARROT ACTION: Begin recognizing the small achievements that move you and your team in the right direction. The momentum you create will help carry you toward your ultimate goal. And if it means you coming in with your stomach painted blue, well, all we'll say is Go team!

A Talent a Day

Discover their hidden strengths.

⌒

Take the time to find out what skills or hobbies or previous-life experience the people around you possess. Then, pick a day to focus on one person and one thing, whatever it may be. On your break, ask Frank to show everyone how he ties flies. Let Angie have her day in the sun by explaining hydroponic tomato gardening. People will be fascinated by Quinn and his coaching of a women's roller-derby team. Seriously.

And don't buy too much into the stereotypes either. The women in the office won't mind devoting fifteen minutes one day to hear the finer points of base-stealing, and the men can devote one break to learning about scrapbooking. When we spend just a few minutes a day appreciating the multifaceted talents of the members of our team, we not only promote camaraderie, but we are able to identify hidden strengths in our people.

CARROT ACTION: Get to know the people you work with a little better by taking just one break a month to showcase an employee's hobby or proudest accomplishment outside of work. Discovering hidden strengths always makes you a better co-worker, boss, or friend.

The Ride Is Free,
and It Is the Reward

Life is just a journey.
—Princess Diana

A study by psychologists at Emory University revealed that cash does not create happiness. In fact, these experts said that sudden wealth, particularly for people who did not work for it, such as lottery winners, does not stimulate lasting happiness.

Often times, when people are asked to define their goals, they respond by saying something like, "I want to be rich." However, though money can be perceived as a measurement of success, it appears that it does not provide fulfillment if it has not been earned.

Instead of viewing money as a goal, view it as a measurement tool. Focus on your purpose, your passion, and the goals at hand. Master your craft. Create timelines. And simply count the dollars as one aspect of your reward instead of the goal itself.

CARROT ACTION: Money pays bills. Instead of dreaming about having money, define your wants and desires according to your passions.

Two Wrongs

No one has ever recognized me.

⌒

Two wrongs don't make a right (though three rights do make a left). If you were never recognized, that is regrettable, but it doesn't mean those around you should be cheated, too. Start watching and congratulating co-workers on their unique contributions.

CARROT ACTION: Make up for past slights and make sure your teammates don't feel that way, too.

Active Change

*Success in life isn't based on your ability
to simply change . . . [but] to change faster
than your competition, customers, and business.*
—Mark Sanborn

Death and taxes are certain. So is change. In business, everyone knows that the ability to respond to change is critical. It's the ability to create change that's magical.

Your life, your job, your family, your physique, your relationships, and the world around you will inevitably change. Your job is to respond in positive ways, seeing change as an opportunity rather than a challenge.

Here's one example. When the portable music market seemed to be passing Apple by, Steve Jobs hired an expert team that brought them the revolutionary iPod—changing the music industry forever. Jobs knew that those who can hold themselves accountable for creating change will be leaders. The rest will just cross their fingers, hoping it all works out in the end.

CARROT ACTION: Beat the clock. Forecast the changes in your world that will occur in the next six months and become accountable for your future. Create your change.

Noise

What you do speaks so loud that
I cannot hear what you say.
—Ralph Waldo Emerson

The most powerful words are those that are never spoken. When you cross your arms, nod your head, frown, smile, or gaze off into the distance, your audience hears everything you do, but may not ever hear everything you say. Because of this, it's just as important to focus on your communicative actions, postures, and nuances as it is to hone your vocabulary—otherwise your words will be drowned out by nonverbal noise.

Keep in mind that "noise" constitutes any action, even those that do not match the words you speak. Contradictory actions, overt actions, and a lack of action or expression can all be extremely noisy to any conversation.

CARROT ACTION: Practice your new "noiseless" communication in front of a mirror or with a close friend. Note what messages you are sending with your body.

In the Midnight Hour

Less is more when it comes to after-hours emails.

Stephanie is chief information officer for a security firm. She loves her job, works long hours, and is always thinking of new ways to improve upon herself and the company's product. She had a habit of emailing ideas to employees and senior leaders all day and night, and even on weekends.

The staff loved having Stephanie on the team, but they didn't appreciate the "off the clock" emails. For instance, she would often send "must do" lists to her team on Friday or Saturday evenings. And, although she intended the emails as reminders for Monday morning, the team—even other late-night emailers—perceived the notices as a request to work through the weekend.

Be mindful of your influence and intent when you send emails after hours. Your recipients—even the ones who also email you at odd hours—might view the communication differently than you do.

CARROT ACTION: Push the pause button. If you have ideas that hit you during the weekend or at 2:00 a.m., write the email, but don't send it until the workday has begun.

Ripple

How far does your voice reach?

A Phoenix woman never realized, when she sent out a message on Facebook telling her friends to conduct self-examinations for breast cancer, that one of her contacts' lives would change forever. Her contact heeded her advice and found a lump. As a result, she immediately found treatment.

Too often we hold our tongues, withhold advice, and monitor our concerns simply because we believe no one is listening.

When do the sound waves created from your voice end? Quite possibly, only when you stop speaking (or, in the above case, typing).

CARROT ACTION: A word of thanks, concern, insight, or information can travel further than you might imagine. Speak up. Never put yourself in position of regret, thinking "if only I had said something."

What's Crazy in Your Life?

*Not caring how others feel is an attitude for losers—
that can only lead to less and less effectiveness.*
—Jim Kouzes and Barry Posner

Sometimes we get so caught up in our work—deadlines, projects, budgets—that we don't take the time to think about those who are helping us accomplish those goals.

Our team members need our attention. In fact, if we take a spark of interest in their lives, our work situations will typically improve. We certainly will have people more willing and motivated to help us reach those deadlines, excel at the projects, and stay within budget.

CARROT ACTION: Give a Carrot today in the form of talk. Ask your co-workers about anything but the job. Try: "What are you passionate about right now outside of work?" If your co-worker starts talking about the job, so be it. At least she knows you care enough to ask.

Hold Onto This

I can live two months on a good compliment.
—Mark Twain

We were once told by an enlightened man: "I've discovered you don't need recognition very often. Just during the weeks you eat."

Food keeps our bodies alive. Recognition feeds our egos, minds, and souls. It's what keeps us going, trying, and achieving. You should be recognizing someone with some form of specific recognition every week. Finish this sentence in front of someone great at work, "You know what I really like about your work style . . ."

CARROT ACTION: For a strong and healthy team, provide a steady diet of recognition. Just as with fruits and vegetables, try offering up five compliments a day.

Un-Birthdays

It's just an excuse to really be nice to someone.

Designate a certain day once a week as Jennifer Day, Peter Day, or Susan Day. And yes, of course you have to pick an actual person on your team.

Pick someone and make it his or her day. You don't have to get too extravagant, but here are some ideas: tags for everyone to wear with an interesting factoid about the person; take five minutes out of a staff meeting to go around the room and say something nice about him; put his face on the bulletin board; give him the best parking space; decorate his cube . . . you get the idea. Treats of some kind are nice, but in this case, it's truly the thought that counts.

CARROT ACTION: It doesn't have to take a lot of time or money, but the payoff for really paying attention to someone will pay dividends. Friendships, culture, and productivity are all given a boost. This week, identify five people to recognize in this way.

What About Me?

Remember the unremembered: mother,
father, spouse, children, hamster.

Sure, Steve is doing a fantastic job with the new custom solution (and you better let him know it), but what about Steve's wife and kids who are suffering from dad's late nights, early mornings, and distracted weekends?

Get the team together and have them write a card or put a care package together for Steve's family with things such as food, flowers, movie tickets, and a thank you card. A kind word or thought to the home support team can do wonders for their attitudes, and watch what it does for Steve!

CARROT ACTION: You don't need to spend a lot of green to get results with this one. A sincerely worded card and some inexpensive treats for the kids can go miles.

E-Oops

Can email haunt you forever?

Often, an email mishap is nothing more than embarrassing—a bit of blushing the instant after you hit send. However, worse things have happened. Your message could be entered as evidence in a lawsuit

A good rule of thumb is to treat every email, incoming or outgoing, as formal correspondence. Always keep in mind that the email could be forwarded to anyone, and could potentially be retrieved years after you send it.

CARROT ACTION: Never email when you're emotional—it's too easy to toss statements into the world that you might regret later.

I Spy

It is not enough to believe in recognition,
you have to behave like you believe in it.
—Eric Harvey

Someone is watching you. In fact, *every one* of your team-mates is watching you.

So many of us believe that we're invisible, that we can walk through the organization and no one will know what we are up to on a daily basis. But your co-workers watch you, talk about you, and study you. They have a PhD in *you*.

That's why it's so important that your walk is in sync with your talk. Whether you are a leader or a team member, be transparent—open, and honest with everyone around you. The impact will be long-lasting.

CARROT ACTION: Think of ways your actions contradict your professed belief in recognition. Set specific goals to bring the two into closer alignment.

Carrots Basics Reminder

Personal

Let's say you want to thank a work associate for covering for you while you took a family leave. You could go to HR or your manager and ask for the standard lunch certificates or movie passes, but maybe this time around you'll do something more personal.

While "personal" isn't technically one of the three pillars of effective recognition (frequent, specific, timely), it's right up there. When and where possible, select Carrots that will have some level of personal impact on or significance for the recipient.

How well do you know the co-worker? Are you aware of her likes/dislikes, hobbies, interests, family, appetites, obsessions, addictions, and vices? Okay, that may be too much information, but what about her favorite snack food or dessert?

In any form, personalizing the gift speaks of your true appreciation.

CARROT ACTION: Get to know your associates better. Pay attention to what they talk about at lunch. Take a good look at their workspaces, and the pictures and doodads they adorn them with. You'll soon get a clear idea of what they'd appreciate getting from you.

E-motion

*Electric communication will never be a substitute
for the face of someone who with their soul
encourages another person to be brave and true.*
—Charles Dickens

Remember the look on your mother's face the first time you tried to make a grilled cheese sandwich in a toaster (or something equally misguided)? Her expression, that piercing angry glare, her folded arms, which made you tremble with fear?

She couldn't have shown that level of disappointment with instant messaging. A note saying, "Hey knucklehead, that wasn't very smart," just doesn't have the same effect.

The same is true for positive communication. Your enthusiasm and appreciation for people is simply not expressed to its fullest extent through an impersonal email or instant message. For praise, use your voice—a higher form of communication.

CARROT ACTION: Hang a post-it note on your computer that reads, *If I want to communicate emotion, I must let them hear me or see my genuine expression of gratitude.*

Turn It Around

Attitude changes mistakes into learning opportunities.

A wise saying goes: "Experience comes from good judgment; but good judgment comes from bad experience."

We all make mistakes—from blowing a design decision to buying a pair of parachute pants. Try admitting your blunders to colleagues and brainstorming ways to avoid another mistake going forward.

This approach has many benefits: (1) Employees will be impressed by your candidness and honesty; (2) they will be prepared to avoid the same mistake themselves; (3) they will feel safer admitting mistakes to you in the future (rather than trying to cover them up); and (4) they will feel freer to be innovative.

CARROT ACTION: Turn your next mistake into a team-building moment by acknowledging your error to colleagues and thinking up ways to avoid the mistake again. Show others that they are in a supportive environment.

Yesterday

How's it working for you?
—Dr. Phil

In our hectic work lives we don't have much time to reflect on the past. But we'd like to take the time now to encourage some reflection. You've been reading these daily messages for quite some time now, and some of them focus on holding yourself accountable. So, consider this entry a test. Review the past five pages of this book. Pick one of the Carrot Actions that you followed through on. Then, subject yourself to our Doctor Phil impersonation: "How's it working for you?"

For those of you who are feeling overwhelming guilt about something undone, get over it. We're giving you a second chance to hold yourself accountable. Implement the Carrot Action below, and do it with passion, vigor, and pride.

CARROT ACTION: Tell one person today how much you appreciate them, and specifically *why* you appreciate them.

If You Ain't Using It, Donate It

Can they put it to better use?

⌐⌐

Sometimes the best gift is the gift of time. If you can swing it, arrange for a half-day off for someone on the team, perhaps an early out on Friday. Or, if you're willing and if your company will let you, how about donating a vacation day to someone you value? Chances are, if you haven't used it, you won't, and it can be a great motivator/relief for someone who *really* needs it.

A long weekend can be just the thing to recharge someone's batteries. Thankful for your sacrifice, they'll make great use of their time when they come back to work. And when you need a favor returned? Count on it.

CARROT ACTION: Make your donation even cooler by making a "presentation" at work. Let everyone else know why this person deserves what she's getting. Have her announce her plans.

Dress Down

Recognition in denim.

Have a casual Friday to recognize a significant team accomplishment. You can learn a lot about an individual by the clothes he or she chooses to wear to be comfortable. And they'll get to know you better, as well.

Even the most traditionally conservative environments can relax once in a while, boosting familiarity and team morale.

CARROT ACTION: As a team, determine an appropriate goal to shoot for—it should take no more than a month to accomplish—and work to achieve it so that you can dress down.

E-gads

Too little or too late can send a powerful message.

Electronic communication has its pros and cons. However, one huge communications-related danger is not responding to a potentially destructive email.

Let's face it; many of us receive dozens if not hundreds of emails daily, and most of the emails will never be read because they are selling something we don't want or from someone (a Nigerian "prince") we don't trust. Others are work-related but ask for a response that, quite frankly, you don't know how, or don't feel comfortable enough, to answer.

Lack of response, even in email, is a response. And, because the email you received lives eternally somewhere out there in cyber space—your too little, too late response could come back to haunt you.

CARROT ACTION: We know you're busy. However, there's a simple element of recognition that we rarely talk about, but which needs clarification. All relationships, even those in cyberspace, are based on respect. Take time, at least, to recognize the communication you receive from those important to you. A simple, "Got your message. Will get back to you ASAP," is often enough to show you are thinking about their request.

Get Read

How to make sure your emails get read.

⌒⌒

We're all bombarded with so many emails that some of us read only those with intriguing subject lines.

If your emails aren't getting responses, or replies are slow to come, try changing your subject line to something the recipients don't expect, or to one that will draw immediate attention.

Standard subject: Important policy amendments
New, subject: Stay out of trouble with accounting . . . in three easy steps.

You can also hold your reader's attention in the body of the email by hooking the content to a payoff at the end.

Standard intro: There is a new policy amendment concerning HG102.
New intro: This email will be about as fun as reading your insurance policy, but it's worth it.

CARROT ACTION: Effective written communication means that your audience actually reads it. Today, step away from "professional" a bit, and lean more towards "edifying."

Caped-Goats

Do you have a hero who's shouldered the blame?

Nathan was just four years old. He was a well-behaved child—polite, loving, and pretty calm for his age. However, Nathan had a friend from preschool named Jay. Jay was a spirited kid, with more energy reserves than a barrel of monkeys.

Nathan's and Jay's personalities complemented each other; one was calm and the other vigorous. When Jay spent afternoons in "time-out," Nathan would console him.

Then, one day, Nathan was feeling a bit rambunctious himself. When nobody was looking, he knocked over the Lego tower built by some other boys in the class.

The preschool teachers couldn't believe Nathan would do something so malicious and devious.

"I did it," said Jay. And Jay took the penalty despite his innocence.

Do you know someone who's taken ownership for a mistake with a client or senior leadership, even though it wasn't all her fault? Maybe she deserves some appreciation as a team hero—accepting accountability for others' actions.

CARROT ACTION: It's time to pay your dues. Without confessions or causing a scene, spread some positive news today about the person who has taken ownership for a problem he didn't have to. It's karma. It'll all come back.

Become Barbara Walters

How interviewing can boost performance.

There's a big issue when it comes to communication—some people withhold details they think others won't find important.

How many times have you been working on a project and late in the game found out that there was a big piece of information that would have helped you along the way? How many times have you worked with a colleague and years later discovered that he, too, is a fan of Dean Martin, and suffer from chronic nightmares about Big Bird?

Interviewing is an effective way to understand your colleagues, their roles and capabilities, and their personality drivers.

It may seem odd at first, but go tell a colleague. "I'd like to learn more about what you do because there may be a way we can help each other."

Act like Barbara Walters for fifteen minutes, asking questions such as "What is your favorite childhood memory?" "If you could choose any profession in the world, what would it be?" The value is tremendous.

CARROT ACTION: Create a schedule to interview each of your team members for just twenty minutes. Ask them about work preferences, as well as things outside of work.

Be Careful What You Reward

The behavior will be repeated.

Rewards are effective only when they honor the right people for the right behaviors. Here's an example of a reward nearly gone wrong. (We changed the names to protect the guilty.)

A vice president sat down with his CEO and a list of his customer service directors. The VP had ranked them from one to six. When asked what the ranking involved, he said, "Susan's number one. She gets the new business packets out in the fastest time. They are always very neat."

"Who gets their packages out in the most creative, manner, helping us win the most accounts?" the CEO asked.

The VP said, "That would be Roger."

Guess where Roger ranked? Near the bottom. His stuff wasn't so neat and on-time, but he closed like a demon.

If the CEO had approved the bonuses without consulting his VP about his decision-making process, management would have rewarded the wrong things? The message to Roger and his team would have been: Work faster. Be neat. We don't care about winning accounts. *Ouch.*

CARROT ACTION: Be careful what you reward, because it *will* be repeated. Next time you are about to hand out a reward, ask yourself if the behavior furthers your team's raison d'etre.

Carrots for Life

Bring it home.

⌐⌐

A manager at a large tire manufacturer once told us how it bothered him that his boss was a despotic, mean-faced bully at work, but, according to neighbors, *away* from work he was a charming, delightful, life-of-the-party type guy.

We also heard a story of a woman who was bright, funny, and gracious in the boardroom, but often demeaning and insensitive to her family at home.

The point here is to be the best *you* at work, at home, or wherever you are. If you have developed a mastery of Carrots among your co-workers and they would describe you as thoughtful, kind, respectful, and generous, isn't it only fair that you bring that wonderfulness home to the people who matter most?

CARROT ACTION: Take note of the way you treat others at work today and how you resolve issues, then apply the same solutions tonight at home. Or, tonight, take note of how you treat your family, and make sure to bring that attitude to work on the morrow.

Vertical Chatter

Kiss Down. Talk Up.

Two negative terms have greatly defined the way many people communicate with one another at work. The first term is *kiss up*. The second term is *talk down*.

Kissing up to our superiors is common practice—a tactic used to further advance our standing. *Talking down* is common for leaders and those with experience—a tactic that makes subordinates feel small and insignificant. True leaders are born when people choose to follow them, and these leaders advance their careers by focusing their positive attentions down or sideways rather than up.

Kiss up to follow.

Kiss down to lead.

CARROT ACTION: Pucker up. Today make someone feel great who is below your level in the organization.

Above the Call of Duty

How you spell top performer.

Create an A-B-C-D award to be given to a person on your team who always goes Above and Beyond the Call of Duty. We were visiting a pharmaceutical company one day when an A-B-C-D award was being presented to a cheerful customer service rep who had a knack with difficult customers. Teammates spoke of her ability to turn a negative into a positive, and told stories of angry customers spending more money with them by the time their phone calls were over.

CARROT ACTION: Since we learned our ABCs in school, the award could be a reminder of our school days—a basket of fresh apples, a huge gold star . . . or a stuffed carrot.

Fashionably Late

Making an entrance or creating a reputation?

What does your arrival time communicate to those who are expecting your presence?

- **Early:** shows you respect the people who are expecting you (unless you're too early, which can be perceived as disrespect).
- **On time:** reveals that you understood and respect the agreement made previously, as well as the people you're meeting.
- **Late:** shows that you don't care about the other party's needs or time.

Fashionably late is actually a faux pas in business.

CARROT ACTION: Show those around you that you respect their time, and expect that they will respect yours. Recognize the people who always show up on time—not because they're dying to work with you or be with you, but because they're showing you respect.

Textiquette

Quick and easy can appear sloppy and vague.

Communication technology allows us to conduct business and maintain consistent communication in our personal relationships no matter where we are in the world. Text messaging even allows us to conduct two conversations at the same time—how many meetings have you attended where everyone in the room is talking to one another but still texting or emailing someone else at the same time?

It's time to remember our "textiquette" (text etiquette, as we call it).

1. Realize that the people you're meeting with might be offended that they don't have your full attention.
2. Realize that even though the person you're texting might have texted you first, and you want to send an immediate response, you might not know your recipient well enough to use abbreviations and marginal grammar/spelling.

CARROT ACTION: If you're in a meeting with someone who is texting and you want their full attention, it may not be necessary to cause a scene. Simply wait for them to come up for air and politely get them in the discussion.

Name Names

Share the credit in public.

When you give a presentation to senior management or a speech to a trade group, be sure to acknowledge everyone on your team who worked on the topic you are addressing—by name. This type of recognition shows management you are a team builder who is willing to share credit. Inevitably, word will leak back to your people that you support them and are looking to build their careers, too.

CARROT ACTION: When will you next be presenting to a group? Build a slide with the names and faces of those who helped you.

Accepting Criticism

Injustice anywhere is a threat to justice everywhere.
—Dr. Martin Luther King, Jr.

Criticism can hurt. It can build walls, create resentment, and even create feuds. Yet sometimes we need to hear it. It can make us better, stronger, and wiser.

How should we appropriately accept criticism?

Step 1: Analyze your critic's intention. Although your feelings might be hurt, your critic probably isn't purposely trying to make you feel bad.

Step 2: Validate your critic's feelings and concerns. You can't argue with someone else's feelings. They are always justified.

Step 3: Use the criticism—whether you agree with it or not—as a tool for self-improvement. For instance, maybe the critic says you're disengaged or disinterested, but really you're just not a chatty person. How can you appear more interested?

CARROT ACTION: Want to fight criticism with criticism? Rethink your approach to a critical personality. If someone is being unjustly critical of you, try being overwhelmingly positive about his efforts. Many times people criticize most the people they fear will be the most critical of them.

Go There

*Go as far as you can see,
and when you get there you will see farther.*

Philosophers have long pontificated about the unknown. But we don't need to dig deep to realize that our goals of today are starting points to our next goals. For everything we do, accomplish, and aspire to reach, there is a first time. And, when we succeed we look for the next challenge, not to repeat the first.

High school graduation doesn't lead us to wonder if we could repeat the grades again, it leads us to continued education. Entry level jobs don't lead us to parallel jobs, they lead to career advancement. Ask any athletic record-holder if she thinks she could repeat her performance. All of them will get a smug look on their faces, look you square in the eye, and tell you that they have set a new goal to beat their previous record.

CARROT ACTION: Instead of meeting the expectations of your bosses, set a goal that's seemingly out of reach. When you arrive at that goal, you'll see an entirely new perspective of possibility. Go there. And, see what happens next.

A Roomful of Flowers

Say it with a hundred roses.

Want to say congratulations in a spectacular way? Send one hundred roses home or to the office to celebrate a promotion or exceptional job. It may sound corny, and of course you've got to be careful not to overstep boundaries, but we've seen it done and the reaction can be spectacular. In one case, an executive team sent one hundred flowers to the wife of a newly promoted director. The man had been traveling a lot and the note with the flowers expressed sincere appreciation for the family's support as well as their congratulations on his promotion. The next day she sent an email to each member of the executive team. Her note in part said, "You sure know how to make a gal cry . . . My husband works hard, but surprises like this make it all worthwhile."

It looks great, feels great to receive, and smells great—the elusive trifecta of recognition*.

*Legal disclaimer: Great-smelling is actually not critical to effective recognition, nor is there such a thing as an "elusive trifecta of recognition." Void where prohibited. Not available in parts of Iceland or Vermont.

CARROT ACTION: There are several online flower brokers that provide this service at very affordable prices. It's a once-in-a-lifetime experience that your team won't forget.

Succeed. Repeat.

Reaching a small goal is easy. Repeat again.

Kelly was determined to lose twenty-five pounds. She bought the latest diet book, but never read it.

A year went by, and Kelly now wanted to lose thirty pounds. She saw an ad for the newest diet book, bought it, read the first chapter, realized that she wasn't motivated enough to read the next, and the new book was shelved.

Another year went by. Kelly's class reunion was coming up. She was focused on losing thirty-five pounds. She bought the brand new diet book, read the whole thing, and began seeing the weight fall off her body. First it was five pounds, then ten. By the time her class reunion arrived Kelly had lost seventeen pounds—an impressive loss. But she refused to attend because she felt like a failure. And she quit the diet the very next day.

Point #1: If you buy the book, follow the instructions.
Point #2: If you see progress, don't stop. Enjoy your success and keep going.

CARROT ACTION: Choose a small Carrot Action from this book that you feel created a successful outcome. It doesn't have to change the world, just make it slightly better. Tomorrow, repeat again. Hey, it worked, why stop?

A Handshake

*The right to be heard does not automatically
include the right to be taken seriously.*
—Hubert Humphrey

In some ways it's sad that the agreement handshake has been replaced by legal documents and contracts. Corporate scandal makes headlines daily. Corruption seems to be an expectation within at least a small percentage of the business world.

Today's world is different than our parents' world. Our parents would tell us that a man or woman "is only as good as their word." But today, our words are only as good as the people who speak them.

It's time to start acting as if our promise is our handshake, that our word is sealed and guaranteed by a contract. Trust must be earned—through action not argument, because actions are the only things that that truly communicate the truth.

CARROT ACTION: Recognize someone today simply for following through on a promise.

No Budget?

Anyone can afford to recognize.

We all wish we had unlimited funds to appreciate others (or to build a villa in Tuscany). But recognition doesn't have to cost a lot. Remember, it is how you make people *feel* that is important. A stack of thank-you cards costs pennies. Certificates can be printed for next to nothing on a color printer. An email to the boss or an announcement of achievement costs nothing.

CARROT ACTION: Get creative. Gather co-workers together and whiteboard a list of fifty creative recognition ideas for each other. Then think about specific ideas for specific people. The more you put into the idea the more it will mean to those who receive it.

Trick or Treat

Celebrate the season.

With enough advance notice and permission you should be able to appropriately enjoy a little "dress up." Many companies we work with confess that they encourage employees to wear costumes, wigs, and makeup now and then during the year, not only on Halloween

Select an appropriate theme like political characters, movie stars, historical figures, or, even better, people at work, i.e., your boss, the head of HR, the CEO, or anyone else with enough of a sense of humor to allow themselves to be mimicked.

Party at lunch or later in the afternoon, bring plenty of snacks and drinks, and enjoy one another's fun side.

Events, parties, and celebrations are all varieties of Carrots that continue to build up truly satisfying cultures.

CARROT ACTION: Run it past your boss and head up a small committee to plan the party.

C U Text 2

Nifty, convenient, but not always effective.

⌒

At lunch the other day we overheard some nurses stuck somewhere in between a conversation with one another and the people they were text messaging.

"She wants to know when we'll be back," one said. "OMG, a break would be nice. BRB." Yes, she really spoke those abbreviations. "LOL, she's the biggest baby."

You get the point.

Technology is a fantastic tool for communication, but it also eliminates many of the subtleties that help us understand one another. Humor is dangerous in emails. Emotion is marginalized in text messages. And sarcasm—as proved in the above LOL—is completely lost.

When given the opportunity, communication is most effective in person, still effective on the phone, but diminishes as you move down the electronic media.

XOXO just doesn't have the same appeal in a text message. Get face to face when you need to make a point or clarify.

CARROT ACTION: Lead with technology, follow with face-to-face. Use text messages to say, "I want to talk to you, stop by when you get a chance." This allows the recipient to fit you into his schedule, but still gives you the face time you desire.

Turnaround

Sending it right back at ya.

The next time you're recognized, be sure to thank the person who recognized you. Accept the praise without false modesty, but then be sure to acknowledge her kindness in noticing your achievement.

CARROT ACTION: When you are praised or rewarded next, send a handwritten note of thanks expressing why his acknowledgement of your achievement meant so much.

Survivor

Success seems to be largely a matter
of hanging on after others have let go.
—William Feather

∿

Reality television shows always have sensational competitions. They test physical skills, smarts, or your "gross" factor—are you willing to eat goat intestine, stand in pool of volcanic lava, or allow nine rattlesnakes and seventeen scorpions to slither over you; all while a cranky English fellow tells you that your singing voice is atrocious?

But there's one test on reality television that every contestant seems to have a fair shot at winning: the test of will power.

As crucial as it is to develop our skills and hone our talents, sometimes the most successful person is simply the one who outlasts the competition.

CARROT ACTION: Most goals require timelines. However, choose one goal in your life for which you're willing to outlast all your competitors.

Optimism

I can't change the direction of the wind,
but I can adjust my sails to always reach my destination.
—Jimmy Dean

Some goals are hard to visualize. Some dreams seem too distant to reach. Some destinations seem beyond the horizon. But if Columbus hadn't sailed, if Edison hadn't imagined, if the Wrights remained grounded, if Ford hadn't built a process, if Michael hadn't moonwalked, and if you can't believe, goals are meaningless.

Everything is impossible until it's possible. Have faith in your ability to achieve what seems unattainable.

CARROT ACTION: Remove the word "if" from your vocabulary. Replace it with the word "when."

When Certificates Work

Improving relationships with this gift.

We are not big fans of gift certificates. There are too many land mines. For example, many times employees don't redeem them—a boon to the gift certificate company—and other times employees are offended by the meager amount they are given.

However, even though we've expressed our dislike, now and then, a personalized gift certificate can be thoughtful. For example, a great reward for a new homeowner is a gift certificate to a home-improvement store. For someone else, a gift certificate to a favorite restaurant could show thoughtfulness. To make this reward effective, you need to know your co-workers' likes and dislikes, and a little about their personal lives. If you have your finger on the pulse of what's important to them outside of their work lives, you might just find an appropriate reward.

CARROT ACTION: When you give a gift certificate, it must be applicable and appropriate.

Steady Action

Thinking well is wise; planning well, wiser;
doing well wisest and best of all.
—Persian proverb

In the fable about the Tortoise and the Hare we learn the great lesson that putting one foot in front of the other, no matter your speed, is the most effective means of securing success.

Business and cultural icons prove this premise time and again. Bill Gates introduced a product that many scoffed at: who would want a personal computer in his living room? J. K. Rowling's book about a wizard named Harry Potter was rejected countless times before publication. And Greg Mortenson, an economically challenged mountain climber from Minnesota, envisioned building schools for children in northern Pakistan before making his dream a reality and writing a bestselling book. All were considered "dreamers." But, like the tortoise, they placed one foot in front of the other, and kept going.

Leaders lead even if no one is following. They act on their ideologies. They hold themselves accountable to make their dreams realities.

They don't always have perfect ideas or plans but they do have perfect action—forward movement.

CARROT ACTION: Recognize someone who has a dream today. Your support may be the push they need.

Do Business, Not Busyness

Focusing on quality versus quantity.

Todd sold air time for a radio station. He had a theory that the more companies he could reach each day, the more sales he would make.

But this plan didn't prove to be successful, so, as the months went by, Todd found himself working later than ever.

Finally, Todd's manager said that he was impressed by his work ethic, but that the results had to get better or else. Defeated, Todd went home to plan a new strategy, realizing that he might soon get fired from his job. The next morning he decided to approach some of the clients he had already called on. But instead of selling them radio advertising, Todd gave them the best advertising ideas he had for their businesses—even if those ideas didn't include a budget to buy radio ads.

That month, Todd broke the all-time sales record, and, of course, kept his job. The point: It may be time to look at old problems with a new twist. In this case, worrying less about the sale and more about helping a customer.

CARROT ACTION: Be accountable for your outcomes. Track your daily tasks in one of two categories that relate to your overall goal: (1) urgent, and (2) important. Today, just do those things that are urgent. Tomorrow, hit the important list.

Keeping On

The virtue of endurance.

The greatest composer of classical music in America is a very old man.

On the occasion of his one-hundredth birthday in 2008, Elliott Carter sat in Carnegie Hall to hear his newest work, *Inventions*, composed for piano and orchestra. After the performance, a birthday cake was wheeled out. Carter strolled forward to acknowledge the thunderous applause. He joked that he'd finished the new piece before the commission was due, "just in case."

Unprecedented in the history of music, Carter is still writing brilliant, complex works. No first-rate composer has ever had such a late blossoming.

At the end of the day, who wouldn't want to still be relevant when your peers are long gone? But how to make it happen?

Endurance trumps everything. But the greatest achievement is made by those who not only survive in their jobs, but who also build their life's work to a crescendo as they age.

CARROT ACTION: How do you picture yourself in old age? If you imagine a significant decline in some area of your life, strengthen it now to prepare.

Appreciate Smart Ideas

Your brain doesn't hold all the answers.

It's not your job to have all the answers. But it *is* your job not to let the good ones get away.

Some people ask us why their teams never seem to generate new and innovative ideas, why their groups seem to stagnate in mediocrity. We tell them it's because employee ideas are not appreciated.

Start a suggestion box, dedicate part of weekly staff meetings to idea generation and, of course, publicly recognize people for their ideas.

An energy company we worked with implemented a suggestion program a few years ago and accelerated the results with recognition. They thanked each employee who submitted an idea with a small award. If the idea was accepted the person received another thank you. And finally, if the idea was implemented that employee received a commensurate award. In the first year seven thousand ideas were generated, resulting in $16 million in savings for the corporation.

CARROT ACTION: Remember that recognizing innovative ideas—not just achievements—fosters creativity within the workplace. After all, each and every employee wants to feel that they are making significant contributions in their workplaces. It's up to you to make sure they do.

Great Operators

How may I direct your call? No problemo.

⌐⌐

The power of recognition knows no bounds. People outside your team, group, or division need a little love as well. How about that operator answering phones in a little office in the back. Finding busy executives, handling interested customers, fending off solicitors. There's not always a lot of camaraderie for the busy operator. Give him or her a boost by showing up with a little brilliance. In this case, brilliance can be translated thus: cookies.

Alone, or, better, in a group, the presentation of the treats will make a big impression.

CARROT ACTION: Who else is in the building but not "in the group"? Unfortunately, cliques don't die with high school. Make an effort to include someone.

Pick Up Some Slack

But don't call them slackers.

⌒⌒

If you've ever had too much work to do (like the last two years), then you know how great it feels to have a meeting, assignment, or requirement canceled or pushed back. It gives you a little breathing room, hence: sanity, hence: better productivity. The same feeling comes when a co-worker offers to help.

Give a co-worker some sanity by offering to take something off of his plate. Ask what's on his list, and what you can take from him. It may be as simple as giving him the comforting knowledge that someone's got his back. Whether you take over for him or collaborate, this sort of thing has a way of coming back to you.

CARROT ACTION: If you think you're busy, just watch someone else for a while.

Bumper Stickers

Whenever two good people argue over principles,
they are both right.
—Marie Ebner von Eschenbach

Bumper stickers are rarely neutral when it comes to expressing opinions. In fact, many are geared to inflame an opposing viewpoint—poking at political or college affiliation, religious belief, or social movement. And, as much as some of those statements might ruffle our feathers, the opinions and communication of those opinions accomplish a lot—we all come to understand or better clarify our own beliefs in the process.

In business, sometimes our "bumper stickers" on important business issues are hidden due to fear of upsetting the status quo. Sometimes ideas remain unexpressed, perspectives untapped, and opinions dismissed. In the process, we lose the great possibility of better understanding differing viewpoints on issues that could affect our future.

CARROT ACTION: Recognize someone who shares her opinion, even if you disagree with that opinion. Thank her sincerely and ask questions to clarify your understanding. Honest, open communication leads to possibilities.

Know Again

The celebration of one success launches a thousand more.
—Adrian Gostick and Chester Elton

The word "recognition" has two parts—"cognition," or "to know," and "re" which means "again." When you recognize something, you are reliving through story an event that has taken place by "knowing it again."

We learn from past events. Not only that, but people repeat behaviors that are recognized. Public recognition motivates everyone in the room to do more of what spawned the award. In this way, recognition becomes a catalyst for increasingly on-track, above-and-beyond performance.

CARROT ACTION: During your next award presentation, tell a story about the award winner to "know again" their accomplishment.

Tale of the Tape

Nothing holds man accountable more than video.

It's always shocking to watch the first few episodes of a new season of *American Idol*. Many contestants are horrible singers, raising the question: haven't they ever recorded themselves?

Singing in the shower is one thing—we may actually believe we sound decent with bubbles in our ears—but most of us know that when we record ourselves, even just our speaking voices, we're not happy with what we hear.

With other recording mechanisms, the truth is similarly revealed. And, not only is it revealed, but it becomes a tangible thing, something that can be passed on to other people so that they can learn the truth about you as well.

Aside from audio and video it's important to record our actions in writing; otherwise we can't accurately measure our progress, our talents, and our weaknesses.

Without recording, we too may end up facing the music at some point, when the truth is revealed to a much bigger audience than just ourselves.

CARROT ACTION: Not all of life can be planned, but it all can be recorded. On your way to your goal, make sure to record your efforts in a journal nightly. Tonight is a perfect time to start.

Words that Move Us

Words are the most powerful drug used by mankind.

Why do Little League coaches praise their players? "Nice work getting down in front of that grounder, Billy." "Good eye, Leah." "Nice bruise, Thomas!"

Words translate into emotions, and emotions drive human behavior. Watch what happens the next time you recognize a team member for a job well done, a significant other for supporting you, or a child for an accomplishment.

Words drive behaviors because people want to be recognized for their talents, pursuits, and successes.

CARROT ACTION: Even though you might *think* the people around you know how much you appreciate them, make a point to recognize someone special today. Choose your words carefully, using descriptive verbs and nouns that you know will motivate.

Sixty-Second Praise

Creating a great moment in a minute.

All the time takes to make someone's day, using on-the-spot recognition, is sixty seconds. The next time you notice an employee doing something right, go through the following steps:

1. Tell her exactly what she did that was right ("Tess, I noticed that you picked up the phones today, since Andy was sick.")
2. Tell her what value or goal she met. ("That shows a lot of teamwork.")
3. Explain how her meeting the goal impacts the company. ("We might have missed that emergency call from our biggest customer without your help.")
4. Express appreciation. ("Thanks so much.")

CARROT ACTION: In less time than it took you to read this page, you can recognize someone—go take a walk and find a worthy employee now.

Self-Victory

The first and best victory is to conquer self.
—Plato

It's easy to point fingers, unless we're pointing them at ourselves. While more difficult than blame, self-accountability is critical to success and necessary in the pursuit of business accomplishment.

What could you improve about your relationship with team members, bosses, or employees? What about those who drop the ball during your climb to the top? Think about how you could inspire or motivate team members better. Think about ways you could help them achieve so the entire organization achieves.

Once you've mastered all the areas where you can improve, and helped others succeed, victory will be yours. You'll not only feel more fulfilled, but you'll most likely have achieved pecuniary success as well.

CARROT ACTION: Do a self-assessment survey. Ask yourself: Do I take initiative, report regularly on my progress to my boss and co-workers, resolve problems, and care about others around me? You may learn critical things about yourself that you hadn't considered before.

Mind Games

A man must get a thing before he can forget it.
—Oliver Wendell Holmes

On the path to achieving your goal, it's important to establish a system of reminders to maintain your focus. Let's face it; we're all human. We're forgetful, often distracted, and could use a little help in the memory department. Planners, organizers, and PDAs work well to organize our must-do lists. But the old-school ways work too—a string around your finger, a note in your pocket, or a quick doodle on your hand.

Choose a reminder system that works for you. Stay focused; it's essential to your success.

CARROT ACTION: Set a reminder to yourself to do something nice online for a friend or colleague today. Write them a Linkedin recommendation, write a blog on their amazing abilities, mention them on your Facebook page, or send them a posting you think might be of interest to them.

No Such Thing as a Free Lunch

Unless you pay for them.

Do you have one of those extra-frugal people on your team who never goes out to lunch with the group because "it's not in the budget"? Times are always tight for someone, but lunches are a great way to blow off steam, to talk anything other than shop, and to build friendships.

So, offer to buy someone lunch. Get them out of the office. It's amazing the things you learn about them. And vice versa, see how that works? They'll also be grateful you asked.

Now, some people's pride may get in the way: "I don't take no handouts ya'll." So you may have to get sneaky about it and offer it in the form of a gift certificate.

CARROT ACTION: Start with a smaller group, and let this person get acclimated to group activities. And remember: bonding can happen over tacos just as easily as steak.

One a Week

Avoid mass praise like the plague.

When planning recognition, some neophytes worry about offending an employee or leaving someone out. So they opt to recognize everyone as a group. These folks not only end up alienating the stars that make a difference, but *reinforcing* the behavior of their average and poor performers.

Instead of serving up mass praise to your work group, try this: put together a chart of your team members and recognize one person in each weekly staff meeting until you have publicly recognized them all. Don't just recognize for "overall greatness," but for specific behaviors that are important to you and your organization.

CARROT ACTION: Unless you are walking the floor every day, it's impossible to see how each person is contributing to the goals of the organization. Whether your team is remote or all in the same office, spend at least half an hour a day among your teammates. This way, you'll soon be recognizing the right behaviors on the spot. And best of all, you'll notice teammates recognizing each other, as well as vying for more of your recognition.

All the Powers of the Universe

In an eight-by-ten-inch space.

〜

Every company has done the employee of the month award. Near the thirtieth, phrases like, "Whose turn is it?" can be heard around the executive offices.

Random recognition has no power and no purpose. It's every bit as de-motivating as recognition done right is motivating.

If your company insists on keeping the monthly award, then make it better. Along with that eight-by-ten of his smug mug on the wall, how about writing a letter to him about something awesome he did to deserve the honor? And you might also gather everyone together to publicly congratulate the person and tell a story about his accomplishment. Letting others know the specifics of a teammate's awesome behavior inspires them to do the same.

CARROT ACTION: Include others' comments as well as your own. Valuing someone else's perspective is recognition in and of itself.

The Old Switcheroo

Rescue a colleague from parking lot Siberia.

If your work building has ever been called a "campus" you are probably part of a pretty large organization. Chances are excellent that parking spaces are doled out based on seniority or position, leaving many of your co-workers to trek long distances to get to the office.

Especially during winter months, consider making your cushy, cozy, upfront parking space a nice little reward for a job well done. For a cube mate or team player who helps make your job easier or just flat out rocks, change parking stalls with them for a week just to say thanks. Who knows? Maybe the boss will catch on and offer to send his limo to pick someone up someday. It *could* happen.

CARROT ACTION: Find out where your co-workers park and see if the switch will make a big enough difference to serve as a reward. If so, single someone out for great work and offer up the switch.

Ownership

No snowflake in an avalanche ever feels responsible.
—George Burns

Somewhere in the world there is a military pilot preparing to fly a critical mission in a fighter jet. On that jet, there is a windshield.

Somewhere else, there is a manufacturing plant that makes military-grade glass cleaner for that windshield. And in that plant is a worker whose job is to ensure that every bottle is free of debris—for a speck of sand could start a crack that could shatter the protective window.

A chain like this could continue eternally—reaching into the worker's household, into his community, and far beyond.

The point is that every link in every chain has the ability to influence something far greater than our imaginations can comprehend. Such is the case with every role in life that we play—at home and in our businesses. Whether through the products we provide, the service we render to others, or simply the smile we offer in the morning, we all make a profound difference to others.

CARROT ACTION: Stretch your imagination and create a fictitious chain of events to see what the possibilities would be if you performed your job/role better or worse today than you normally would. The outcome might help you realize just how important you are.

Heart and Soul

*It's not how much we give
but what we put into the giving.*
—Mother Teresa

Sometimes it's not so much what we say, but how we say it. A sincere thank you doesn't come from a well-written script, but from a sincere heart.

Sincerity is easy when we recognize what matters most in our team. That starts with clear goals and consistent appreciation when someone furthers those goals. Sincerity is rarely polished or saccharine sweet, but is human and warm.

CARROT ACTION: Don't worry that the words aren't elegant, and never let that stop you from giving a presentation or an award; just make sure the warm feeling is genuine.

Ability

Accountability breeds response-ability.
—Stephen R. Covey

Imagine a world or a workplace where accountability doesn't exist—it doesn't matter what you do, when you do it, or how much you produce. Or, even closer to reality in many organizations today, employees, team members, and peers aren't granted the permission to make decisions, and so they're not accountable or responsible for anything except obedience.

What is the potential of a person who has been stripped of accountability and responsibility? How will he or she react to crisis? What will be his motivation? And what if he holds the solution or idea that could revolutionize an organization, or an entire industry?

One CEO told us his company had recently lost a large client. Two hourly employees stopped by the CEO's office the next day. They asked if there was anything they could do to win the customer back. The CEO was floored by their example and ownership. He'll tell that story for years.

CARROT ACTION: Take responsibility for a project that you may find intimidating. Offer accountability to part of the deliverable to a team member who shows special interest in the project. Allow yourself and those around you to rise to their full potential.

Gotcha!

Catch them orange-handed.

⌒

Seems to us, the problem with accountability is that it's always negative. Didn't meet the deadline. Didn't reach the goal. Could've done better.

How about holding people accountable in positive ways?

It takes a little self-training, but, if you keep your eyes open, you'll start to see good stuff happening all around you. As soon as you see it, say something. Big things, little things, try to catch people in the act of good behavior. Reinforce these good behaviors, and they will continue, and spread to others.

CARROT ACTION: Try carrying around a three-by-five card. On one side write down the positive things you say and on the other write the negative. In short order, you'll find out which you focus on and it'll help you tweak your comments towards the positive.

We Are What We Do

*It is not only what we do, but also what we do not do,
for which we are accountable.*
—Molière

In one of his books, executive coach Marshall Goldsmith lists bad habits we need to break at work. The list includes the need to win all the time, the desire to add our two cents in every discussion, making sarcastic or cutting remarks, passing the buck, failing to give recognition, or taking the credit when it's not ours to take.

Taking accountability for our bad habits takes us on a deep journey into the core of who we are. It defines us as a better person.

We are living and breathing products of those things we choose to do, and of those things we choose not to do. Either way, our choices are active. Standing still, goofing off, or running full stride toward our passion are all actions for which we are accountable.

CARROT ACTION: Make a new type of to-do list with everyday actions you want to do more or less of—eat a healthy breakfast, kiss your children goodbye, say thank you, exercise, and so on. Make small steps to do more of the things that lead you to a better place, and less of the things you consider bad habits.

All You Had to Do Was Ask

Never hurts.

Recognition is so many different things to so many people. This is encouraging and daunting. It's encouraging because we can add some personality, it's daunting because we have to add personality.

If you're wondering how someone likes to be recognized or rewarded for his efforts, just ask. Have a conversation. Some people like more responsibility, others time off. Some prefer private vs. public recognition. Some *say* they prefer private, but they'd inwardly love you to get out a megaphone.

Open your mouth and ask. Ask others too. Co-workers, spouses, children, and even bosses can be a wealth of knowledge.

CARROT ACTION: Put together a Recognition Survey. If you don't have one, we published one in our book *The Invisible Employee*. It's a great way to say: "I want to know how to recognize you when you do a great job." Questions for your survey might include: "What's been your favorite type of recognition at work?" or "If you had a day off to do as you wanted, what would you do?"

Face Time

Sometimes the best reward is time with the big cheese.

For many employees, the best reward is knowing that their actions are being noticed by someone in a senior position.

Consider rewarding a great employee by taking her along on your next meeting with senior management. Let the boss know she'll be coming and why, and then speak about the projects the employee is working on and her contributions to your team's success.

CARROT ACTION: Spread the love and you'll not only garner loyalty from your employee, but you'll be seen as a nurturing team player by your bosses.

What's in a Name?

When name calling is a good thing.

We all know when people are faking it: "Hey, you. How are you doing, good looking?"

Make a great effort to remember names. Use people's names when you recognize them, when you praise them, even when you greet them in the morning. Calling people by name is one of the most basic forms of recognition. It shows you recognize them not only as employees but, also as individuals.

CARROT ACTION: Start today. If you don't remember someone's name ask another colleague. Write the names down if you need to. Acknowledge every person you see until you walk out the door tonight.

Enthusiasm

We follow the dynamic.

People tend to be motivated by those who are passionate, even if those people are not the most qualified or the most knowledgeable about the subject. There is something about an enthusiastic attitude that allows us to think and dream a little bigger, and to take a little more risk.

It is a shame that in the workplace we tend to drive passion away. We have become too calculated and too careful. And yet one engaged and enthusiastic team member will spawn another, and then another, until an entire team is ignited. That's when goals are exceeded and game-changing ideas take root.

All of us have worked at one time or other with a person with infectious optimism and energy. Their enthusiasm almost always makes everything better. It boosts creativity and makes work a lot more fun.

CARROT ACTION: If you are passionate about a project, let it show. Express your enthusiasm to team members and assume more leadership.

The Perfect Gift

Holiday giving should be appropriate.

One human resources professional we talked with proudly announced she had ordered pewter bowls for her company's holiday gifts. We asked why, given her largely male, blue-collar employee population. She sighed as though she were talking to misguided seven-year-olds and said, "Because everyone *loves* pewter bowls."

"Oh," we replied.

On our next visit, after a holiday season full of complaints from line workers, she had to admit that perhaps her assumption might have been a smidge off base. She followed up in subsequent years with a selection of items that employees could choose from.

CARROT ACTION: The moral here is: get to know your employees before you buy them holiday gifts. Be thoughtful, and consider offering a selection of items if you can.

Fabulous Shoes

*What your footwear and other accessories
might communicate.*

⌒

We don't consider ourselves fashionistas by any stretch of
the imagination, but we do notice attire from time to time.

Business attire has been the topic of discussion for
decades—what is appropriate, and what might be considered "off-color" (of course, we applaud anything orange).

Fashion, although not considered a requirement for good
business, does influence the way others perceive us, whether
we like it or not. Right or wrong may not be the question.
Rather, the question is: how do you want to be perceived?

Ill-fitting clothing, funky hairstyles, heavy perfume or
cologne, and too many accessories tell the world something
about us, even if it's only the simple fact that we are not
good shoppers.

CARROT ACTION: Understand your audience when picking
attire and always be professional. And always keep something orange on hand if you want to catch attention.

Field Trip

Refuel, renew, and rejuvenate.

Revitalize as a team with a creative field trip to someplace interesting—maybe a museum, or a nearby landmark, or a comedy show. A great reward is to do this on company time, and cover entrance fees.

CARROT ACTION: Taking team members out of their routine lets them rejuvenate so they're refueled and renewed when they return to the office.

Feather the Nest

Onboarding the newbies.

One hospital in the metro Washington, D.C., area reported a high turnover of nurses. Competition for these medical professionals was so intense that a full quarter of newly hired nurses accepted a position but then never started, finding a slightly better deal somewhere else. The organization realized they needed to help everyone feel welcome and engaged even before day one.

Today, before a new hire's first day, he receives a couriered package from the hospital. Inside is a card signed by every member of his team-to-be, welcoming the person and offering congratulations. On the nurse's start date, co-workers gather together for half an hour, enjoying juice, coffee, and doughnuts, but also answering whatever questions the new person has and offering insights into work culture and relationships that may help orient him quicker.

Plant their seeds in your Carrot Culture right away and watch them grow.

CARROT ACTION: Commit to being a work friend and greeting new employees the minute you first encounter them.

More Miles from the Turkey

Make the company gift your own.

Here's a way to be generous without spending a dime. You can get more mileage from the company's holiday gift—whether a turkey, fruit basket, or cash bonus—by personally picking up any of those items and delivering it to your teammates with a handshake and word of thanks for their service over the last year.

Not only is this another way to acknowledge their effort, but it also helps them alieviate another stress of the holidays—picking up their gift from HR.

CARROT ACTION: As you make the rounds with the gifts or bonuses, spend a little time with each person and express sincere gratitude for specific contributions. We guarantee the time invested will be well spent.

Off-Site Activity

Anybody can play kickball.

Getting away from the mother ship and doing things together can be a great way to strengthen your team's unity, whether it's a Friday afternoon movie, a best-ball golf tournament, sports leagues, or barbecues. Look for activities that not only get people out from behind their desks, but which are also conducive to talking and laughing. Encourage your department director to organize a co-ed volleyball or softball team. Kickball for adults is another sport that has picked up steam in recent years. You could also put together a bowling league or take hikes together.

Whatever you do, remember to invite and include everyone. Sometimes it's a good idea to reach out to the techies in the group and plan something around what they like. Maybe a rousing online battle at someone's house or a game of laser tag will bring them around or open them up.

It may be an old saying, but no less golden for its age: A team that plays together, stays together.

Carrot Action: Check with your manager or supervisor to block out a time on the calendar for a team camaraderie activity off-site.

Best Foot Forward

The tales we tell.

⌒

We all have public and private versions of ourselves. There's the face we present to others—for example, the fun-loving guy who can log more work hours than anybody—and the face we see in the mirror in the middle of the night—the guy who's just trying to get through the week in one piece.

There's nothing devious about this kind of dual life. It's simply how many of us live. We're doing the best we can, but it's a lot to juggle.

The hidden truth is that we are all walking around with doubts swirling inside us, and this is one more reason to recognize and celebrate the people around us. Imagine how important it is to any of us, when we're feeling stretched to the limit, to have a colleague say, "Hey, you matter. Thank you."

CARROT ACTION: Today, as you recognize the efforts of someone around you, take a moment afterwards to note how that praise affects them. Watch their posture, the tone of their voice, and their energy.

Hey, Snack Guy!

Keep that bowl full.

Nearly every office has at least one: the generous co-worker who makes weekly runs to the discount warehouse store for bags of candy, gum, or other assorted confectionary on his or her own dime just to share the snacks with everyone else. If you have one such person, be sure to thank him or her today.

However, if your workplace is suffering for a lack of a Snack Supplier, consider nominating yourself or gather a team of associates. It's an easy, low cost team Carrot that keeps people coming to and gathering around your desk. And on days that are dragging by the time the afternoon hits, most people are looking for a little pick-me-up. Be the one to provide it with a smile and watch how it helps build your Carrot Culture, one gumball at a time.

CARROT ACTION: Purchase a bunch of goodies tonight, bring a big bowl from home and place it on your desk tomorrow morning—offer a treat to anyone who stops by to start the ball rolling.

Ease the Squeeze

Set spending limits on your team.

Your team will inevitably want to buy each other gifts at the holidays, but it's a good idea to set a limit on spending. Five to ten dollars is usually sufficient to find something appropriate, and it helps those with tight budgets. Secret Santa, Yankee Swap, and White Elephant gift giving can also be fun ways to spead the love while keeping costs down.

CARROT ACTION: Gather your team together early and ask if everyone wants to exchange serious or cheesy gifts. Letting them know you'll open the gifts at the same time will usually keep everyone on the same page.

The Must-Have Party

Set a time and place and make it happen.

A common mistake of managers is failing to organize a company holiday party. For many of your employees, the best part of the holidays is simply coming together as a group in a more relaxed setting and getting to know team members on a more personal level.

In this economy most managers are strapped for cash. Several leaders we spoke with realized a holiday outing at a fancy restaurant was not in their cards, so they cooked dinner for their employees at their house. Others organized potlucks in the office, with the boss bringing the entrée.

CARROT ACTION: The party doesn't need to be a formal affair at night, and it certainly shouldn't be the wild lampshade-on-the-head shindig you see in the movies. A simple lunch or potluck breakfast is all that is needed to bring people together and create some positive memories. And mistletoe is *so* out.

Soft Cell or Hard Cell

Loudmouth phoners: Praise worthy or craze-worthy.

Who are the so-called experts of cell phone etiquette? Some people will speak at full volume in the middle of a crowd, as if they want the whole world to know how little Jimmy scored 100 percent on his math test. Others will disappear into the corner, as if they were having a clandestine conversation with Batman.

The way we communicate with other callers sends a message: we are focused on the conversation. And the way we handle calls in public sends a message: we respect the people around us.

What's right or wrong? It depends on the culture, though extremes are never a good idea.

Communication requires judgment. Use yours. And by the way, conference us in next time you're on the line with the caped crusader.

CARROT ACTION: Give the people you are with your full attention. When you are engaged in a real conversation with a colleague, client, or employee, avoid looking at your cell phone when it buzzes. We know you are seeing if the person calling is more important than we are, but it's bad form. When you give the person you're currently speaking to the proper recognition, they'll return respect to you.

Thanks Be

The big picture.

According to a broad survey published in the *Washington Post,* some 92 percent of Americans believe in God or a universal spirit. This is quite an extraordinary number if you think about it. Also remarkable: half of Americans say they pray every day, and 80 percent have faith in miracles.

The workplace is typically not the environment for overt religious expression. Tolerance of differing beliefs, including disbelief, helps employees feel safe and accepted on the job. Still, on this day near Christmas time, let's take a minute to think of the big picture.

If there is a higher power, what should our attitude be to that power, especially regarding thanks? The Carrot Principle is all about specific, frequent, and timely recognition. How about recognizing God or a greater power?

Take time to consider the big picture, and give credit to forces that are bigger than you.

CARROT ACTION: Think about what it is you believe in, and then ensure that your actions reflect those core values. Find some time today to be by yourself, to meditate a few minutes, and be thankful.

Smile, Darn Ya, Smile

Grin and bare your teeth.

In good times or bad, the choice is often yours to be happy. Even if, deep down, you're feeling rotten because of life's vicissitudes, you should try your hardest not to mope about, seeking sympathy or a shoulder to cry on.

An old children's song goes:

> If you chance to see a frown
> Do not let it stay,
> Quickly turn it upside down
> And smile that frown away.

Overly simplistic? Maybe. But it's very useful advice. The more you smile the better you'll feel, really, and so will those with whom you interact.

CARROT ACTION: Don't doubt the power of smiling at your work associates. They may think you're nuts, but blow it off, that little smile is like a tiny Carrot seed.

Memories

Light the corners of . . .

Think about how much you love going through old photo albums at home. Isn't it a kick to see the kids in diapers playing in sprinklers, "Patches" when he was a puppy, or even the wedding photos from your *first* marriage?

Putting together a simple photo album or scrapbook celebrating a co-worker's service anniversary is a truly unique gift. A hard-cover, bound version will have the most palpable impact, but don't ignore technology's conveniences. Creating a special Facebook or Web page for your associate is easier and can be shared with many more well-wishers.

Ask HR for old ID photos, look through newsletters, ask colleagues for any shots they have. However you do it, have fun with the project, and, as always, make the scrapbook items specific.

CARROT ACTION: Go to HR or your department administrator to learn the service anniversary dates of your teammates. You may be surprised to find someone very close to you has a milestone just ahead!

Get to Know Me!

A questionnaire

A health care firm we worked with in Alabama sent out a survey to all of its staffers. It asked employees questions designed to help everyone get to know each other a little better.

The survey asked things like, What's your favorite restaurant? Where do you like to shop for clothes? Do you have a favorite sports team—if so, who? If you could go anywhere in the world, where would you go and what are some of the things you would want to do?

Answers were used in a yearbook, but the objective of the questionnaire went beyond merely team building, it also provided managers and co-workers with very practical information that they could use in recognizing someone.

Rather than just handing staff the standard logo-emblazoned coffee mug or ten percent discount in the company cafeteria, management now can award them with a Carrot specifically selected from the answers on their survey. Who knew Rhonda liked bass fishing or Doug dreamed of visiting Greenland?

CARROT ACTION: Work up a form asking the questions that would most help you to recognize someone in a personal, meaningful way, and aim to send it out one week (or two, whichever you think is more appropriate) from today.

Bond, Team Bond

Great teams cheer for each other.

Watch the strong teams in your company. You'll probably notice that the team members encourage each other's accomplishments; each individual is rooting for everyone on the team to thrive. There are few, if any, jealousies. These are teams that celebrate the little individual victories that lead to the entire team's success. They believe we're all in this together.

One of the best ways to build your cohesive team is with Carrots. When you're supportive of your teammates and their successes, it opens the door for them to be supportive of you. Let's help each other succeed.

CARROT ACTION: Our research shows great teams encourage each other. Encourage a teammate today with a sincere, "I'm impressed" or "you're such a great asset to this team." You take the first step and the team will follow.

The Phone

Pick it up.

In age where we can email, text, twitter, and Facebook, we sometimes forget that we can pick up the phone. When there are misunderstandings the best cure can be to hear the other person's voice and talk through the issues at hand. Emails and texts don't give you the inflection and the intent on delicate matters. When in doubt, make the simple decision to just pick up the phone.

CARROT ACTION: Great leaders are great communicators. Make sure you leverage every way you have to communicate clearly. When you are in doubt about the intent of an email, text, or any other communication, don't jump to any conclusions until you have heard the voice behind the electronic missive and talked it through.

The Little Things

Small acts that make us world-class.

At the world's most famous arena in New York City works the world's highest paid trash man.

Scott O'Neil is president of Madison Square Garden Sports. As he walks around the storied arena it is not uncommon for him to stop and pick up a small piece of trash that has landed on the floor. Not only that, he also stops to talk with employees, calls them by name, and never fails to give a word of encouragement.

Scott works eighty hours a week running a sports and media empire. Why would he take the extra time to wander the halls picking up trash and chatting with his co-workers? Because these are the little things that make going to Madison Square Garden a memorable experience. A clean and friendly arena helps create memories that will last a lifetime.

CARROT ACTION: What little things can you do every day that can contribute to creating a world-class workplace? Picking up trash? A kind word? A smile? Find that thing and do it today.

Champions Celebrate

Winners make merry together.

Championship teams celebrate. In sports, when a team wins the World Cup, SuperBowl, or Stanley Cup, they rejoice with parades, parties, and champagne-soaked locker rooms. At the Oscars, Academy Award winners race to the stage and tearfully thank their mothers before running off to grand parties.

So, why don't we celebrate success more at work? Several main objections arise, and they're all misguided: we are busy, it is unprofessional, the project isn't completely done yet, and more.

People are drawn to winning teams. When you celebrate as a group it lets team members know you are of championship quality. It draws talent to your team and excites current teammates for the next win.

CARROT ACTION: Set a department goal and plan the celebration for achieving that goal at the same time. Give your team a collective goal to shoot for *and* something to look forward to when they reach it.

Hard Times

Challenges build team and personal history.

~~

Ask a veteran employee for a few highlights of his career, and an odd thing happens. In the majority of cases, he won't recount periods of prosperity and bliss; rather, he'll tell you about challenges he faced.

It sounds counterintuitive, but we tend to remember hard times more fondly than the easy as we look back on our careers. Tough assignments bring out the best in our characters, even though we might not have enjoyed the challenge at the time. We remember best the ways we overcame the struggles with innovation, grit, and determination, and we are filled with pride in our competence.

The moral? Don't shirk the tough assignments, they shape who we will become.

CARROT ACTION: At lunch with your team today, remember a few of the hard times you've been through together. Let the discussion give you confidence that what you are struggling with now can be overcome as well.

On Call

Impossible choices.

⌒

At a party we were talking to a friend who is a doctor at one of the premiere cancer hospitals in the world. As we chatted, his pager beeped and he looked down at the screen (doctors don't ignore pagers). Suddenly, his faced changed, his shoulders dropped, and he let out a soft sigh. A patient had just died.

"Do you ever feel like you should be doing more?" he asked us. The doctor confided that at any given minute, no matter how hard or long he worked, there were at least four or five places where he was supposed to be, but he couldn't physically be in all of those places at one time.

Everyone feels that way sometimes. The idea of being caught up and on top of things is a shifting mirage. So can we ever feel content?

The key is not to do many things with mediocre intensity, but rather to feel, at the end of the day, that you did something, even if it's just one thing, well. Satisfaction springs from that fact. And that is worth celebrating.

CARROT ACTION: What was the last thing you did really well and said to yourself, "That was a major achievement"? Focus on that thing and work to make it happen again.

Santa's Identity Revealed

Surprises from honesty.

"I'm ready to talk about Santa Claus," Dash said.

Our friend's son Dash was eight years old, and his father always told him that if he really wanted to know the truth about anything, he could come to his father and ask.

"Okay," Dad replied, "What do you want to know?"

"Are *you* Santa Claus?"

He didn't hesitate before he answered, even though he knew there would be consequences for telling the truth. "Yes," he answered. "I'm Santa Claus."

Dash said, "I knew it. I knew you were the man who dressed up and got in a sleigh and delivered toys to everyone around the world . . ."

There are consequences to telling the truth, and they are sometimes unexpected. In the long term, however, honesty brings joy—at home or in the office.

CARROT ACTION: Garner the reputation of a truth teller. Don't do it to be cruel or to intimidate; rather, learn how to be honest and positive and you will see surprising results.

Peace on Earth

Really.

⌒

With any luck, you're not working today. It's Christmas Eve, and hopefully you're getting a well-deserved break. That's not to say, however, that you don't have a thousand tasks to accomplish. We suggest you take a second to think about one thing: on a day that strives to be about peace on earth and goodwill toward all people, where are you falling short?

Is there somebody—a neighbor whose dog barks too often, a snarling clerk at the grocery store, a disgruntled postal worker, an incompetent co-worker, a playground bully, an anonymous driver who scratched your car in the parking lot, a politician whose opinions drive you crazy—for whom you've been harboring ill-will?

Make peace.

You can't fix them, but you can fix your reaction to them.

Every bit of malice you're carrying around with you is emotional dead weight. Today's as good a day as any to shrug it off. Give yourself the gift of peace.

CARROT ACTION: Create this simple list: people for whom you've harbored a grudge. Ask yourself whether that emotion is doing you any good. If not, it's a good day to move on. Try to find something positive that the person does for you and acknowledge it to them.

Just What I Wanted

Recognition that really hits home.

At the end of the holiday festivities, gather your children together to open one final gift: a stack of thank-you cards.

Set aside some time tomorrow to help them compose notes of gratitude to grandparents, friends, and relatives. (If this is a new venture, you may want to give the recipients a heads-up so they don't faint upon receiving the cards.) Learning the lost art of the thank-you note will serve your children their entire adult lives (particularly in leadership roles).

CARROT ACTION: Find good examples of your or your colleagues' handiwork to teach your kids how to craft these notes.

Boxing Day

The original Carrot day.

Do you celebrate Boxing Day?

It's still a holiday in the UK, Canada, Australia, and Hong Kong, but even there, the traditional meaning of the day is slowly being lost. Now, it's a day to shop (or make returns).

But its origins come from English tradition. On December 26, the upper classes of society filled a Christmas box with food and gifts and delivered it to people who were less fortunate. They took the gifts to the laborers who worked on their estates, for example, or to their servants.

Boxing Day was an occasion to celebrate the underappreciated worker. It's the original Carrot day.

CARROT ACTION: We hope you don't need to mark your calendar for the one day a year you'll appreciate workers around you. But many of the workers in our surveys say they receive no recognition at all; Boxing Day's not a bad day to begin.

A Reward to Watch

Are You Ready for Some Football?

Look, there's not much going on at work at this point in the year. The whole world is lost in the reverie of the upcoming new year. Since you're going to be at work anyway, you may as well plug in the TV, hook up cable or satellite, or just fire up the Internet, gather around and enjoy the seemingly endless string of college bowl games (we think there are at least eight hundred by now).

Invite your co-workers to the break room or wherever you can manage, grab some junk food on the way in to work, and celebrate the season. Rose, Sugar, Fiesta, any of the bowls will work.

CARROT ACTION: Find a game and watch it at work as a reward. At least have it on. It's a great way to celebrate another year of progress.

Strange Carrots

The fan letter.

⌒

By now you are most likely more adept at recognizing people in your work life and private life than when you started reading this book. You're comfortable showering kind words and creative awards on people. That's great. Hopefully, you've witnessed the creation of a Carrot Culture people prospering in the soil of appreciation.

But are you assuming that carrots should be doled out only to people you know? What about strangers?

You might also consider finding ways to appreciate people you've met but don't know well, and especially those you maybe have never seen: the grocery store employee, yes, but also the farmer who makes your food. The neighborhood firemen rightly deserve recognition, but so do the families of their fallen brothers.

Expand your circle of recognition.

In this interconnected age, it's not difficult to track down contact information for the distant strangers you could praise. Imagine the farmer reading your letter: "We've never met, but I had to drop you a note to say that your carrots are the best in the world. Many thanks!"

CARROT ACTION: Write a note to somebody you've never met but admire. Write a note of appreciation.

Anonymous Carrots

The pleasure of secret recognition.

The Carrot Principle has an underlying message that personal contact is, in itself, a large component of its success. When we praise a co-worker in specific and timely ways, and we do it personally, she feels great satisfaction and becomes motivated to do even greater things. A bond of trust is formed.

But there's another way to give praise that might not be as personal, but is no less special.

Every once in a while it's fun to do the whole thing anonymously.

Don't overdo it, but sometimes it's great to praise on the sly. Leave an anonymous note on the employee refrigerator: "To whoever cleaned this out: XOXO." Windshields are also great for secret messages: "Joanne, everybody admires how much you do for this place. You're great."

Keep the tone relaxed and not too familiar (don't cross over into stalker territory), but have some creative fun.

CARROT ACTION: Make a plan for a stealth Carrot attack. Look around for a target.

Are We There Yet?

Goal setting for people who hate goals

A certain percentage of the population hates New Year's Day. For many of them it's because they loathe New Year's resolutions. For them, goal setting is merely a step away from disappointment, and their corporate goals are no better.

Let's think of goals in a different way. Make a list of your personal values, the core beliefs that keep you going, and put them somewhere prominent at home and at work. Next, regularly review your values and determine whether your current behavior fully corresponds with what you say you believe. Adjust the two with an eye toward continual self-improvement.

It is unlikely that your core value of "fit into clothes you wore at your high school graduation," is realistic. Rather, keep your goals reasonable, such as "exercise three times a week and eat a healthy lunch."

As for corporate goals, you'll find them easier to get behind if they are connected to your core values. Find a way for them to match up, and you'll see it is like the stars aligning.

CARROT ACTION: Make a list of your core values right now. Jot a few onto a piece of paper. During the day, reflect on additions or subtractions you make to the list.

Once More

Start over and succeed.

Although this book has ended for the year, let it be the beginning of your—and your team's—success through recognition and the Basic Four (set clear goals, communicate openly, build trusting relationships, and hold yourself accountable).

We thank you for taking this year-long journey with us. We hoped you've learned some valuable lessons about the specific ways you can recognize your co-workers and improve the Carrot Culture in your office. May you achieve your highest aspirations this year and in the years to come.

CARROT ACTION: Keep up the good work next year!

The Daily Carrot Principle Resources

Want to benefit from the ideas in *The Daily Carrot Principle*?

Authors Adrian Gostick and Chester Elton have produced five free resources to help you do just that. These resources, inspired by their bestselling book, will help you put the book's ideas into practice in your business and your life.

Visit **carrots.com/resources** to get these free resources.

The Proof Your Boss Needs

Do you work for someone who doesn't believe in recognition? This practical guide will give you Gostick and Elton's insider tips for selling senior leadership on the benefits of appreciation.

The World's Greatest Managers

In this audio lesson, Chester Elton interviews some of the world's most successful CEOs and business leaders. Feel free to steal their playbook to make recognition work in your organization.

Carrot Principle Model

Want an easy reminder of the book's key concepts? Download this reference tool and hang it up near your desk.

A Carrot a Week

You don't have to rack your brain thinking up new recognition ideas every seven days. We provide another 52 practical suggestions on how to provide meaningful recognition.

Global Carrots?

Heading on a business trip? Managing employees from other lands? Learn how to say "thank you" in dozens of languages.

Visit **carrots.com/resources** for these free resources.

About the Authors

Adrian Gostick is the author of several bestselling books on corporate culture, including a *New York Times, USA Today,* and *Wall Street Journal* bestseller *The Carrot Principle.* He also wrote the bestsellers *The Levity Effect* (levityeffect.com), *The Integrity Advantage,* and *The 24-Carrot Manager.* His research on employee engagement has been called a "must read for modern-day managers" by Larry King of CNN, "fascinating," by *Fortune* magazine, and "admirable and startling" by *The Wall Street Journal.*

Adrian's books have been translated into 20 languages and are sold in more than 50 countries around the world. As a leadership expert, he has appeared on numerous national television programs including NBC's *Today Show* and has been quoted in dozens of business publications and magazines.

Adrian is vice president of The Carrot Culture Group, a consulting and training division of the O.C. Tanner Company. Adrian earned a master's degree in Strategic Communication and Leadership from Seton Hall University, where he is a guest lecturer on organizational culture. You can reach him at adrian@carrots.com.

Called the "apostle of appreciation," by the *Globe and Mail,* Canada's largest newspaper, and "creative and refreshing" by *The New York Times,* Chester Elton is author of several bestselling leadership books. *The Carrot Principle* from Simon & Schuster has been a *New York Times, Wall Street Journal,* and *USA Today* bestseller, and *The 24-Carrot Manager* has been called a "must read for modern-day managers" by Larry King of CNN. In 2006, *The Invisible Employee,* from John Wiley & Sons also appeared on the *New York Times* bestseller list. Elton's books have been translated into over 20 languages and have sold about a million copies worldwide.

As a motivation expert, Chester has been featured in *The Wall Street Journal, The Washington Post, Fast Company* magazine, and *The New York Times*, and has been a guest on CNN, National Public Radio and CBS' *60 Minutes*. A sought-after speaker and recognition consultant, Chester is the senior vice president of the Carrot Culture Group, a division of the O.C. Tanner Recognition Company.

Chester has spoken to delighted audiences from Seattle to Singapore and from Toronto to Istanbul. He was the highest rated speaker at the national Society for Human Resource Management annual conference. He serves as a recognition consultant to Fortune 100 firms such as KPMG, Wal-Mart, The Pepsi Bottling Group, and Avis Budget Group. You can reach him at chester@carrots.com.

Carrot Talk

During their travels the authors document the craziest boss stories from around the world, gather the best how-tos on recognition and engagement, and interview some of the world's coolest bosses to provide practical advice on what's working and what isn't. Their blogs are relevant, timely, and often hilarious.

ChesterElton.com

AdrianGostick.com